The Cherry Orchard

ANTON CHEKHOV

A Comedy in Four Acts

The Cherry Orchard

a new version in English
by Jean-Claude van Itallie

Grove Press, Inc., New York

First Evergreen Edition 1977
First Printing 1977
ISBN: 0-394-17017-2
Grove Press ISBN: 0-8021-4095-5
Library of Congress Catalog Card Number: 002461

Manufactured in the United States of America

Distributed by Random House, Inc., New York

GROVE PRESS, INC.
196 West Houston Street
New York, N.Y. 10014

PG
3456
.V5
V3
1977

Cast of Characters

RANÉVSKAYA, LYUBOV ANDREYEVNA, landowner, the owner of the cherry orchard

ANYA, her daughter, age seventeen

VARYA, her adopted daughter, age twenty-four

GAYEV, LEONID ANDRÉYEVICH, Madame Ranevskaya's brother

LOPAKHIN, YERMOLAY ALEXÉYEVICH, a merchant

TROFIMOV, PYOTR SERGÉYEVICH, a student, age twenty-eight

SIMEONOV-PISHCHIK, a landowner

CHARLOTTA IVÁNOVNA, the governess

YEPIKHÓDOV, SEMYON PANTELÉYEVICH, the clerk

DUNYASHA, the maid

FIRS, a valet, age eighty-seven

YASHA, a valet, young

VAGRANT

STATION MASTER, POST OFFICE CLERK, GUESTS, SERVANTS

SCENE: MADAME RANEVSKAYA'S ESTATE

This new English version of *The Cherry Orchard* was first presented by Joseph Papp at the Vivian Beaumont Shakespeare Festival Theater at Lincoln Center in New York City on February 17, 1977. It was directed by Andrei Serban. The actors were Irene Worth, C. K. Alexander, Michael Cristofer, Cathryn Damon, Jon De Vries, William Duff-Griffin, Marybeth Hurt, Raul Julia, Dwight Marfield, Ben Masters, Priscilla Smith, Meryl Streep, George Voskovec, and Max Wright.

Act I

A room that is still called the nursery. One of the doors leads to
ANYA'S *room. Daybreak, just before sunrise. It is already*
May. The cherry trees are in bloom, but it is still cold;
there is a frost on the blossoms. The windows are
closed.

DUNYASHA *enters carrying a candle, followed by*
LOPAKHIN, *with a book in his hand.*

LOPAKHIN: The train is in, thank God. What time is it?

DUNYASHA: Nearly two. It's already light out. *(She blows out*
the candle.)

LOPAKHIN: That train is two hours late. *(He yawns and*
stretches.) And look at me: an idiot. I come on purpose to
meet them at the station, and I fall asleep in a chair.
Ach . . . why didn't you wake me?

DUNYASHA: I thought you'd gone. *(She listens.)* Listen, I think
I hear them.

LOPAKHIN *(listening)*: No, they still have to get the bags, and
all that. . . . *(Pause.)* Lyubov Andreyevna has been

3

abroad for five years. I wonder what she's like now? She certainly was somebody then: kind, and easy going, simple. I remember, I must have been fifteen, my father, God rest his soul, had a bakery in the village; he punched me in the face, my nose was bleeding. We had come here to the house for something, he was drunk. Lyubov Andreyevna—I can still see her, she looked so young then, so thin—took me inside to wash me off, to this very room in fact, the nursery. "Don't cry little peasant," she said. "You won't die. We'll still be dancing at your wedding." *(Pause.)* "Little peasant. . . ." It's true. My father was a peasant, and here I am in a white vest and leather boots. A bull in a china shop. . . . Yes, I'm rich, but that's the only thing that's changed. I have a lot of money, but if you look closely I'm still a peasant, nothing more. *(He riffles the pages of the book in his hand.)* Here I was reading this book, and I didn't understand a word. I was reading and I fell asleep. *(Pause.)*

DUNYASHA: The dogs have been barking all night. They know the mistress is coming.

LOPAKHIN: What's the matter with you, Dunyasha? You're so . . .

DUNYASHA: My hands are trembling, they're shaking. I think I'm going to faint.

LOPAKHIN: You're too delicate, too refined, Dunyasha, all dressed up like a lady. Look at your hair. It's not right. You have to know your place.

> YEPIKHODOV *enters carrying a bunch of flowers. He wears a jacket and brightly polished high boots that squeak with every step. As he enters he drops the flowers.*

YEPIKHODOV *(picking them up)*: Here, the gardener sent these.

He said: put them in the dining room. *(He hands* DUNYASHA *the flowers.)*

LOPAKHIN: And bring me some *kvass*.

DUNYASHA: Yes, sir. *(She goes out.)*

YEPIKHODOV: There's a frost this morning. Three degrees of frost, but the cherry trees are in bloom. I can't say I exactly approve of our climate. *(Sigh.)* No. It's not exactly conducive . . . and, permit me to append, Yermolay Alexeyevich: I bought these boots for myself the day before yesterday, and I venture to assure you they squeak to a point that's quite unfeasible. What should I grease them with?

LOPAKHIN: Go away. You bother me.

YEPIKHODOV: Every day something terrible happens to me. But I don't complain. I'm used to it. I just smile.

DUNYASHA *enters and serves* LOPAKHIN *the kvass.*

YEPIKHODOV: I'm going. *(He bumps into a chair which falls over.)* There. *(Triumphantly)* You see? Excuse me for saying so but that's the sort of thing that happens to me . . . all the time . . . it's remarkable . . . just remarkable. . . . *(He goes out.)*

DUNYASHA: You know, Yermolay Alexeyevich, Yepikhodov has proposed to me.

LOPAKHIN: Humph!

DUNYASHA: I don't know what to tell him. He has such nice manners. But, sometimes when he starts talking I don't understand a word. It sounds nice, it's touching and everything, but it doesn't make any sense. I sort of like him, and, of course, he loves me madly. But he's so clumsy, so unlucky. Every day something happens to him. Every day. People tease him; they call him twenty-two misfortunes.

LOPAKHIN *(listening)*: I think they're here.

DUNYASHA: They're coming! What's the matter with me? I'm trembling all over. I'm cold.

LOPAKHIN: Yes, it's them. Let's go meet them. I wonder if she'll recognize me. It's been five years. . . .

DUNYASHA *(excitedly)*: Oh, I'm going to faint, I'm going to faint.

> *We hear two carriages drive up to the house.* LOPAKHIN *and* DUNYASHA *hurry out. The stage is empty. We hear noises from adjoining rooms.* FIRS, *who had gone to the station to meet* LYUBOV ANDREYEVNA, *rapidly crosses the stage, using a cane. He wears livery in the old style, and a top hat. He is talking to himself, but we don't understand what he's saying. From offstage the noise grows louder. A voice says "Let's go through here."* LYUBOV ANDREYEVNA, ANYA, *and* CHARLOTTA *enter. They are wearing traveling clothes.* CHARLOTTA *has a dog on a leash.* VARYA, *who has entered with them, wears a coat and a kerchief. They are followed by* GAYEV, SIMEONOV-PISHCHIK, LOPAKHIN, DUNYASHA *with a bundle and an umbrella, and servants with baggage. All pass through the room.*

ANYA: Let's go through here, Mamma. Do you remember what room this is?

LYUBOV ANDREYEVNA *(joyously through her tears)*: The nursery.

VARYA: It's so cold. My hands are stiff. Mamma, your rooms are just the way you left them, the white one and the lavender one.

LYUBOV ANDREYEVNA: The nursery, my darling precious room! I slept here when I was a child. *(She cries.)* And I am still a child. . . . *(She kisses her brother, then* VARYA, *then her brother again.*) And Varya is just the same: she looks like a nun. And Dunyasha. I recognized her, didn't I? (*She kisses* DUNYASHA.)

GAYEV: The train was two hours late. Two hours! What kind of management is that?

CHARLOTTA (*to* PISHCHIK): And my dog even eats nuts.

PISHCHIK (*amazed*): Just think!

They all go out except ANYA *and* DUNYASHA.

DUNYASHA (*helping* ANYA *with her coat and hat*): It feels like you've been away for so long.

ANYA: I couldn't sleep for four nights on that train, and now I'm freezing.

DUNYASHA: You went away just before Easter; it was snowing and cold. And now look. My darling! (*She laughs and kisses her.*) I've been waiting for you. My joy, I have to tell you something. I can't wait another minute.

ANYA (*wearily*): What is it this time?

DUNYASHA: Yepikhodov, our clerk, proposed to me right after Holy Week!

ANYA: You always tell the same story. (*Rearranging her hair*) I've lost all my hairpins. (*She's exhausted and can hardly stand.*)

DUNYASHA: I don't know what to do about it. He says he loves me, he loves me so. . . .

ANYA (*looking through the door into her own room, tenderly*): My own room, my window; it's as if I'd never been away. I'm home, and tomorrow morning I'll get up and run out into the orchard. Oh, if I could only sleep. I couldn't sleep the entire trip. I was too worried.

DUNYASHA: Pyotr Sergeyevich arrived the day before yesterday.

ANYA (*joyfully*): Petya!

DUNYASHA: He's asleep in the bathhouse; he's staying there. "I don't want to be a bother," he said. (*She glances at a watch which she pulls out of her pocket.*) I would have woken him up, but Varvara Mikhalovna said not to. "Don't wake him up," she said.

VARYA *enters. She has a bunch of keys at her waist.*

VARYA: Dunyasha, coffee quickly. Mamma wants coffee.

DUNYASHA: Right away. (*She goes out.*)

VARYA: Thank God, you've come back. Thank God, my darling is home. My little angel is back (*holding* ANYA).

ANYA: You don't know what I had to go through. . . .

VARYA: I do know. I can imagine.

ANYA: When I left, Easter week, it was so cold, and Charlotta never stopped talking and doing her magic tricks. Why did you have to saddle me with Charlotta?

VARYA: You couldn't have traveled alone, darling. Not at seventeen.

ANYA: It was snowing when we got to Paris . . . and cold. My French is awful. Mamma lived on the fifth floor. I walked up. There were French people in the room: some ladies and an old priest with his prayer book. The place was full of smoke; it was dismal. When I saw Mamma I felt so sorry for her. I hugged her and I held her head in my arms. I couldn't let go of her. Then she held me, and kissed me, and cried.

VARYA (*almost crying*): Don't tell me any more. Don't.

ANYA: She already sold her villa near Menton. She had nothing left, nothing. And I didn't either. Not a kopek. We had hardly enough to come home on. And Mamma doesn't realize. In all the station restaurants she orders what's most expensive, and tips each of the waiters a rouble. Charlotta did the same. And so did Yasha. He demanded whole dinners for himself. It was awful, just awful. You know, Yasha is Mamma's butler now; she brought him home with us.

VARYA: I saw him, the scoundrel.

ANYA: And what about here? Have you paid the interest on the mortgage?

VARYA: With what?

ANYA: Oh, my God. My God.

VARYA: In August the entire estate is going to be sold.

ANYA: Oh, my God.

LOPAKHIN (*sticks his head through the door and moos like a cow*): Mooo. (*He disappears.*)

VARYA (*through tears*): Oh, I'd like to hit him. (*She shakes her fist toward the door.*)

ANYA (*embracing* VARYA *softly*): Varya, did he propose? (VARYA *shakes her head, no.*) He loves you . . . talk to him. Why wait?

VARYA: Because nothing is going to come of it, that's why. He's too busy; he has no time to think of me. He doesn't even know I'm alive. Well, so, that's too bad. I don't want to see him any more. Everyone talks to me about our marriage, congratulates me, but there's nothing. It's only a dream. . . . (*In a different tone*) You're wearing a new brooch. It's a bee, isn't it?

ANYA *(sadly)*: Mamma bought it. *(She goes toward her own room and speaks gaily now, like a child.)* Do you know what? In Paris I went up in a balloon.

VARYA: My angel is home. My precious has come back. *(DUNYASHA has come in with a coffee pot and is preparing the coffee. VARYA is near the door.)* As I work every day, darling, taking care of the estate, I dream, I dream if only we could marry you to a rich man, then I'd feel at peace. I could visit monasteries, go to Kiev, to Moscow. I would travel, all the time, from one holy place to another, on and on. . . . What bliss.

ANYA: The birds are singing in the orchard. What time is it?

VARYA: It must be three, time for you to go to bed, darling. *(She goes into ANYA's room.)* She's home. What bliss.

    YASHA *enters with a lap robe and a traveling bag. He crosses the stage airily.*

YASHA: May I pass through, *s'il vous plait?*

DUNYASHA: We hardly recognized you, Yasha. You look so European.

YASHA: A-hem. And who are you?

DUNYASHA: When you left I was no bigger than this. *(She indicates with her hand.)* I'm Dunyasha, Fyodor Kozoyedov's daughter. Don't you remember me?

YASHA: A-hem. A little peach. *(He looks around. Then he quickly embraces DUNYASHA who cries out and drops a saucer. He runs out the door.)*

VARYA *(annoyed, from the doorway)*: What's going on in here?

DUNYASHA *(tearfully)*: I broke a saucer.

VARYA: That's a good omen.

ANYA *(coming out of her room)*: We have to warn Mamma. Petya's here.

VARYA: I told them not to wake him.

ANYA *(dreamily)*: It's been six years now since Papa died. And only a month after that, Grisha drowned; darling baby brother, he was only seven. Mamma couldn't bear it; she went away without looking back. *(She shivers.)* I know how she feels. She doesn't know I do, but I do. *(Pause.)* And Petya was Grisha's tutor. He'll remind her. . . .

> FIRS *enters wearing a jacket and a white waistcoat. He busies himself with the coffee urn.*

FIRS: Madame will have her coffee here. *(He puts on white gloves.)* Is the coffee ready? *(To* DUNYASHA *sternly)* And you! Where's the cream?

DUNYASHA: Oh, my God. *(She hurries out.)*

FIRS *(fussing with the coffee pot)*: Nincompoop! Good for nothing. *(Muttering to himself)* The mistress is back from Paris. . . . In the old days the master used to go to Paris too, only he went by carriage. . . . *(He laughs.)*

VARYA: What are you laughing at, Firs?

FIRS: Miss? *(Joyfully)* My mistress is back! She's home! She's home! I haven't waited for nothing; now I can die. *(He cries with joy.)*

> LYUBOV ANDREYEVNA, GAYEV, SIMEONOV-PISHCHIK, *and* LOPAKHIN *enter.* PISHCHIK *is wearing a long sleeveless peasant vest made of fine cloth and full Russian trousers tucked into his boots.* GAYEV, *as he comes in, mimes the motions of a billiard player with his hands and elbows.*

LYUBOV ANDREYEVNA: How does it go now? Wait. . . . I remember. Cue ball into the corner! Pot the red!

GAYEV: Cut shot into the corner! Do you remember, Sister, when we were children? We both slept here. And now I'm fifty-one, strange as it seems. . . .

LOPAKHIN: Yes, time flies.

GAYEV: What?

LOPAKHIN: Time flies.

GAYEV: There's a smell of cheap cologne in here.

ANYA: I'm going to bed. Good night, Mamma. *(She kisses her mother.)*

LYUBOV ANDREYEVNA: My darling little girl. *(She kisses her hands.)* Are you glad you're home? I still can't believe it.

ANYA: Good night, Uncle.

GAYEV *(kisses her face and hands)*: God bless you. You look just like your mother. Lyubov, you looked exactly like her.

  ANYA *shakes hands with* LOPAKHIN *and* PISHCHIK, *goes out, and closes the door behind her.*

LYUBOV ANDREYEVNA: She's so tired.

PISHCHIK: It was a long journey.

VARYA *(to* LOPAKHIN *and* PISHCHIK*)*: Well, gentlemen, it's after three. Time to go.

LYUBOV ANDREYEVNA *(laughing)*: You haven't changed, Varya. *(She pulls* VARYA *toward her and kisses her.)* Let me finish my coffee, and then we'll all go. (FIRS *slides a cushion under her feet.)* Thank you, my dear. I drink coffee now. I got used to it in Paris. I drink it day and night. Oh, thank you, my dear old soul. Thank you. *(She kisses him.)*

VARYA: I'd better see if all the luggage is in. *(She goes out.)*

LYUBOV ANDREYEVNA: Is this really me sitting here! *(She laughs.)* I feel like waving my arms and jumping for joy.

(She buries her face in her hands.) But what if it's only a dream? Oh, my God, I love my country; I love it so. On the train I could hardly see out the window, I was crying so much. *(Almost crying)* But I must drink my coffee. Thank you, Firs, thank you, my dear. I'm so glad you're still alive.

FIRS: The day before yesterday . . .

GAYEV: He's going deaf.

LOPAKHIN: I have to go now. At five this morning I have to leave for Kharkov. Poor me. But I wanted to see you, talk with you again. You're as beautiful as ever.

PISHCHIK *(breathing heavily)*: More. She's more beautiful. *Encore plus belle.* And in her Paris dress . . . I'm hers forever. *Je suis à elle pour toujours.*

LOPAKHIN: Your Leonid Andreyevich, your brother here, says I'm an oaf, a peasant, a boor, but I don't care. Let him talk. I only want one thing: that you should trust me as you used to. That your wonderful tender eyes should look at me the way they used to. Dear God, my father was a slave of your grandfather's and your father's, but you, yourself, did so much for me once that I've forgotten all that. And I love you, as if you were my own sister . . . more than my sister. . . .

LYUBOV ANDREYEVNA: I can't sit still. Not now. *(She jumps up and paces back and forth in the room, very moved.)* I can't bear this joy. . . . Laugh at me, I'm silly. My dear bookcase *(she kisses the bookcase)*, my own little table . . .

GAYEV: While you were gone Nanny died.

LYUBOV ANDREYEVNA *(sits again and drinks her coffee)*: Yes, God rest her soul. They wrote and told me.

GAYEV: Anastasy is dead too. And cross-eyed Petruschka left me and is living in town now, working for the police inspector. *(He takes a box from his pocket and sucks on a candy.)*

PISHCHIK: My daughter, Dashenka . . . sends regards.

LOPAKHIN: I would like to tell you something that would please you, cheer you up *(looking at his watch)*, but now I have to go, there's no time . . . well, only two or three words. You know already that your cherry orchard has to be sold to pay your debts, and the auction is set for the twenty-second of August. But don't worry, my dear, you can sleep in peace. There's a way out. Listen carefully: this is my plan. Your estate is only thirteen miles from town, right? The railroad passes nearby, so if you divide the cherry orchard and the land along the river into cottage sites, and lease the sites to summer residents, you'll have, at the very least, twenty-five thousand roubles a year.

GAYEV: Forgive me, but that's nonsense.

LYUBOV ANDREYEVNA: I don't understand you, Yermolay Alexeyevich.

LOPAKHIN: Ask at least twenty-five roubles a year for each two-and-one-half-acre plot, and if you hurry and advertise now, I'll bet you won't have a single piece of land left by fall; it'll all be sold. You'll see. I congratulate you. You're saved. The site is beautiful, the river deep enough to swim in. Of course it will be necessary to rearrange things, tidy up the place. . . . For instance, tear down all the old buildings, including this house which isn't worth anything . . . and cut down the old cherry orchard.

LYUBOV ANDREYEVNA: Cut down the cherry orchard? My dear, excuse me, but you don't understand. If, in the entire province, there is a single remarkable place, it's *our* cherry orchard.

LOPAKHIN: It's remarkable only because it's big. In fact, it bears only once in two years, and even then there's nothing you can do with the cherries; nobody buys them.

GAYEV: But even in the encyclopedia they mention our cherry orchard.

LOPAKHIN *(consulting his watch)*: There's no other way. If you don't decide, the cherry orchard, the whole estate, will be sold at auction on the twenty-second of August. Make up your mind. There is no other solution. None. Absolutely none.

FIRS: In the old days, forty or fifty years ago, they picked the cherries; they dried them, soaked them, and made them into jam. Then they used to—

GAYEV: Firs, be quiet.

FIRS: Then they used to send them by the cartload to Moscow, and Kharkov . . . and that brought in the money. The cherries in those days were soft and juicy, and the smell . . . they knew how to do it then . . . they had the recipe.

LYUBOV ANDREYEVNA: Well, what is the recipe?

FIRS: It's forgotten; nobody remembers.

PISHCHIK: And what about Paris? How was it? Did you eat frogs?

LYUBOV ANDREYEVNA: I ate crocodiles.

PISHCHIK: Just think!

LOPAKHIN: There used to be only landlords and peasants living in the country, but now summer residents are moving in. And all the towns, even the smallest, are surrounded by summer cottages. In twenty years very likely the summer resident will be enormously multiplied. All he does now, of course, is drink tea on his front porch, but maybe one day he will cultivate his own acre, and then the cherry orchard will become a happy, rich, and productive place.

GAYEV *(indignant)*: What nonsense!

Enter VARYA *and* YASHA.

VARYA: Mamma. There are two telegrams for you. *(With a key from her ring she opens the old bookcase. Her keys jingle.)* Here they are.

LYUBOV ANDREYEVNA: From Paris. *(She tears up the telegrams without reading them.)* That's all over.

GAYEV: Do you know how old this bookcase is, Lyuba? A week ago I pulled out the bottom drawer, and I saw the date burned into it. It was made exactly one hundred years ago. What do you think of that? We could celebrate its centennial. I know it's only an inanimate object, but still, it's the bookcase.

PISHCHIK *(surprised)*: A hundred years old! Just think.

GAYEV *(lightly touching the bookcase)*: Yes. . . . Now this is a bookcase. Dear honored bookcase, I salute you. For more than a hundred years your existence has turned our minds toward the bright ideals of goodness and justice. Your silent call to fruitful work has never faltered. *(Through tears)* You have upheld our family courage for generations, our faith in a better future. You have nurtured our ideals of goodness and social consciousness. . . .

Pause.

LOPAKHIN: Yes.

LYUBOV ANDREYEVNA: Still the same Leonya . . . the same as ever.

GAYEV *(a little embarrassed)*: Cannon off the right. Cut into the side pocket.

LOPAKHIN *(glancing at his watch)*: Well, time for me to go.

YASHA *(handing a pill box to* LYUBOV ANDREYEVNA): Would you care to take your pills now, madame?

PISHCHIK: Take no medicines, *chère madame.* They do no good, and they do no harm. May I have them please? *(He takes the pill box from her, empties the pills into the palm of his hand, blows on them, swallows them, and washes them down with kvass.)* There!

LYUBOV ANDREYEVNA *(startled)*: You're mad!

PISHCHIK: Swallowed them all.

LOPAKHIN: What a digestive system! *(All laugh.)*

FIRS: When his honor came to see us during Holy Week, he ate half a bucket of salted cucumbers, all by himself. . . . *(Mutters.)*

LYUBOV ANDREYEVNA: What is he saying?

VARYA: He's been muttering like that for three years now. We're used to it.

YASHA: It's age.

CHARLOTTA IVANOVNA, *looking very thin, tightly corseted, wearing a white dress, with a lorgnette at her belt, crosses the stage.*

LOPAKHIN: Excuse me, Charlotta Ivanovna. I haven't yet had a chance to welcome you. *(He tries to kiss her hand.)*

CHARLOTTA *(pulling her hand away)*: If I let you kiss my hand, then you'll want to kiss my elbow, and then my shoulder.

LOPAKHIN: I'm out of luck today. *(All laugh.)* Charlotta Ivanovna, show us a trick.

LYUBOV ANDREYEVNA: Yes, do show us a trick, Charlotta.

CHARLOTTA: No, I'm going to bed now. *(She goes out.)*

LOPAKHIN: We'll see each other then in three weeks. *(He kisses* LYUBOV ANDREYEVNA's *hand.)* Goodbye till then. I have to go. *(To* GAYEV*)* Goodbye. *(He shakes hands with* VARYA *and then with* FIRS *and* YASHA.*)* I don't feel like leaving. *(To* LYUBOV ANDREYEVNA*)* Think it over, about the summer cottages. When you've come to a decision, let me know. I can find you a loan of fifty-thousand. Think it over, seriously.

VARYA *(angrily)*: Well, if you're going, then why don't you go?

LOPAKHIN: I'm going, I'm going. *(He goes.)*

GAYEV: Oaf! Boor! Oh! I'm so sorry. He's Varya's fiancé, isn't he?

VARYA: Don't talk nonsense, Uncle.

LYUBOV ANDREYEVNA: But Varya, dear. I'd be very happy. He's a good man.

PISHCHIK: A very worthy man. . . . And my Dashenka says— she says lots of things. . . . *(He snores, but wakes up at once.)* Dearest lady, do me a favor—a loan of two hundred forty roubles. Tomorrow the interest on my mortgage must be paid.

VARYA *(frightened)*: No, no, there's no money.

LYUBOV ANDREYEVNA: That's true. I don't have any.

PISHCHIK: I'll find it somehow. Never lose hope. Just when I think it's all over . . . that I'm ruined . . . lo and behold the railroad crosses my land, and they give me money. Anything can happen. . . . Something will turn up, if not today, tomorrow. . . .

LYUBOV ANDREYEVNA: Coffee's finished. Now we can go to bed.

FIRS *(brushing* GAYEV's *clothes, admonishing him)*: You've put on the wrong pants again. What am I going to do with you?

VARYA (*softly*): Anya's asleep. (*She quietly opens a window.*) The sun is up; it's getting warm. Look, Mamma, how beautiful the trees are. My God, the air . . . and the starlings are singing.

GAYEV (*opening another window*): The orchard is all white. You didn't forget it, Lyuba, did you? That long path stretching out there like a ribbon shining on moonlit nights. You thought of it, didn't you? You couldn't forget it.

LYUBOV ANDREYEVNA (*looking out the window*): Oh, my childhood, my innocence. . . . I slept in this room. I awoke every morning, happy, looking out at the orchard, and it was always just as it is now; nothing has changed (*she laughs with joy*): white, all white. After a dark and rainy autumn and a cold, cold winter, my orchard, here you are young again, full of happiness. The angels have not deserted you. . . . Oh, if only I could lift this weight from my heart, and forget the past.

GAYEV: Yes, and now the orchard is going to be sold to pay our debts, strange as it seems.

LYUBOV ANDREYEVNA: Look! Our darling Mamma. Walking through the orchard, in her white dress. (*She laughs with joy.*) It's Mamma. There she is!

GAYEV: Where?

VARYA: Mamma, dear, God be with you.

LYUBOV ANDREYEVNA: There's nobody. I imagined it. Down there on the right, where the path goes off to the summer house, there's a little white tree bent over; it looks like a woman. (TROFIMOV *enters wearing a shabby student's uniform and glasses.*) Oh, what an orchard! What a wonderful orchard. . . . Those masses of white flowers, the blue sky. . . .

TROFIMOV: Lyubov Andreyevna! (*She turns around.*) I only

want to pay my respects. Then I'll leave. *(He kisses her hand fervently.)* I was told to wait until morning, but I couldn't. . . .

LYUBOV *looks at him, not recognizing him.*

VARYA *(through tears)*: It's Petya Trofimov.

TROFIMOV: Petya Trofimov, Grisha's tutor. Have I changed so much?

LYUBOV ANDREYEVNA *embraces him and cries softly.*

GAYEV *(embarrassed)*: Now, now Lyuba.

VARYA *(crying)*: I told you, Petya, to wait until tomorrow.

LYUBOV ANDREYEVNA: My Grisha . . . my little boy . . . my Grisha . . . my baby.

VARYA: What can we do, Mamma? It's God's will.

TROFIMOV *(gently, through tears)*: Don't, don't. . . .

LYUBOV ANDREYEVNA *(continuing to cry quietly)*: My little boy is dead . . . drowned. . . . Why? Why, my friends? *(Lowering her voice)* Anya's asleep in the next room. I am talking too loudly, making too much noise. But, Petya? You were so handsome. Why have you aged so?

TROFIMOV: On the train a peasant woman said I looked like a shabby moth-eaten student.

LYUBOV ANDREYEVNA: You were only a boy then, a sweet little student, and now: where's your hair? . . . and you're wearing glasses. Surely you're not still a student? *(She goes toward the door.)*

TROFIMOV: I'll probably always be a student.

LYUBOV ANDREYEVNA *(kissing her brother and then VARYA)*: Well, time for bed. . . . You've grown old too, Leonid.

PISHCHIK: So, that's it; it's bedtime. Ai, my gout. I'm spending the night. . . . Lyubov Andreyevna, my soul, if you could . . . tomorrow morning, very early . . . two hundred forty roubles.

GAYEV: A one-track mind.

PISHCHIK: Two hundred forty roubles . . . to pay the interest on my mortgage.

LYUBOV ANDREYEVNA: I have no money, my dear.

PISHCHIK: I'll pay it back, Sweet Lady. . . . An insignificant amount.

LYUBOV ANDREYEVNA: All right. Leonid will give it to you. Give it to him, Leonid.

GAYEV (*ironically*): Oh, of course. Leonid will give it to him. Right away. Why not? An insignificant amount. Hold out your pockets.

LYUBOV ANDREYEVNA: What else can we do? He needs it. Give it to him. He'll pay it back. (LYUBOV ANDREYEVNA, PISHCHIK *and* FIRS *go out.* GAYEV *and* YASHA *are still on stage.*)

GAYEV: My sister still hasn't lost the habit of throwing away her money. (*To* YASHA) Move away, my good man, you smell like a brothel.

YASHA (*smirking*): And you, Leonid Andreyevich, are still exactly the same.

GAYEV: What! (*To* VARYA) What did he say?

VARYA (*to* YASHA): Your mother's come from the village; she's been sitting in the kitchen since yesterday. She wants to see you.

YASHA: So, let her wait.

VARYA: Aren't you ashamed?

YASHA: Who cares? She could have come tomorrow. *(He goes out.)*

VARYA: Mamma's just the same. She hasn't changed at all. If she could, she'd give away everything she has.

GAYEV: Yes. . . . *(Pause.)* If a lot of cures are prescribed for a disease, you know the disease is incurable. I keep thinking of remedies, a great many remedies, which means of course I don't have any at all. It would be a remedy, a wonderful remedy if we inherited a fortune, or married our Anya to a rich man, or one of us went to Jaroslavl to try our luck with our old aunt, the Countess. After all, Auntie is very rich.

VARYA *(crying)*: If only God would help us.

GAYEV: Stop sniveling. Auntie is very rich but she doesn't like us. First of all because my sister married a lawyer, a commoner *(ANYA appears at the door)*, not a nobleman. And you must admit my sister's conduct hasn't been exactly virtuous either. She's good and kind and I love her—she's lovable, but she's weak. No matter how you look at it you have to admit she's loose . . . licentious. You can see it in her every gesture—

VARYA: Anya's here.

GAYEV: What? *(Pause.)* That's funny. I have something in my right eye. I can't see very well. As I was saying, last Thursday when I was down at the District Court . . .

Enter ANYA.

VARYA: Why aren't you asleep, Anya?

ANYA: I can't sleep. I'm restless.

GAYEV: My darling. *(He kisses ANYA's hands and face.)* My child . . . *(through tears)* you're not only my niece, you're my angel. You're everything to me. Believe me, believe me . . .

ANYA: I believe you, Uncle. Everyone loves and respects you, but . . . dear Uncle, you mustn't talk so much, you simply must be quiet. What you were just saying about Mamma . . . about your own sister. . . . What were you saying that for?

GAYEV: I know, I know . . . *(He covers his face with* ANYA'*s hand.)* It's awful. God help me. And today again . . . I made a speech to the bookcase . . . it was so stupid. And I only knew it after I finished, so stupid.

VARYA: It's true, Uncle. It would be better if you didn't say anything. Just keep quiet, that's all.

ANYA: If you keep quiet, you'll see, you'll feel better.

GAYEV: I'll keep quiet. *(He kisses* ANYA'*s and* VARYA'*s hands.)* I'll keep quiet. Only one word, about business. On Thursday I was at District Court, and a group of us were talking, you know, a conversation got started, about this and that, and from what they say, it seems it might be possible to get a loan in order to pay the interest.

VARYA: If only God would help us.

GAYEV: Tuesday I go back, and I'll talk with them again. *(To* VARYA*)* Stop crying! *(To* ANYA*)* Your mother will see Lopakhin. He won't refuse to help her, I know. And you, as soon as you've rested, you'll go to Jaroslavl to see the Countess, your great-aunt. That way we'll attack on three different fronts, and it's in the bag! We'll pay the interest; I know it. *(He puts a candy into his mouth.)* On my honor! I'll swear on anything you want. The estate won't be sold. *(Excitedly)* I swear on my own happiness. Here's my hand. You can call me a bad man, or a man without a heart, if I let the estate reach auction. I swear by my whole being.

ANYA: How good you are, Uncle, and so clever. I feel better now. I'm not worried any more. I'm happy.

FIRS *enters.*

FIRS *(reproachfully)*: Leonid Andreyevich, have you no fear of God, Sir? When are you going to bed?

GAYEV: I'm going, I'm going. You can go, Firs. I'll undress myself. Well, little ones, goodnight. Tomorrow is another day. Time for bed. *(He kisses* ANYA *and* VARYA.*)* I'm a man of the eighties. People now don't think much of that time. But I can say that I have suffered for my convictions. It's not for nothing that the peasants love me. You have to really know a peasant. You have to know how to talk to——

ANYA: You're starting again, Uncle.

VARYA: Uncle dear, be quiet.

FIRS *(angry)*: Leonid Andreyevich!

GAYEV: I'm coming. I'm coming. Go to bed. Double bank shot. Into the side pocket. Pot the white. A clean shot. *(He goes out.* FIRS *hobbles after him.)*

FIRS: Leonid Andreyevich . . .

ANYA: I'm not worried any more, but I don't want to go to Jaroslavl. I don't like my great-aunt. But that doesn't matter. I'm not worried now, thanks to Uncle. *(She sits down.)*

VARYA: We have to get some sleep. I'm going. While you were gone we had some trouble. You know only the old servants are living on the estate now: Yefimushka, Polya, Yevstignei, and, of course, Karp. Well, they began letting people, all sorts of people, stay with them at night. All right. I didn't say anything. Then one day I heard that they were spreading a rumor that I had given orders to feed them nothing but dried peas—out of stinginess, you understand. Yevstignei started that rumor. All right, I said to myself, if that's how it is, just you wait. So I sent for Yevstignei. *(She yawns.)* And when he came I said to him: "How could you say that, Yevstignei? You're a fool." *(She looks at* ANYA.*)* Anichka. *(Pause.)* She's asleep. *(She leads* ANYA *by the arm.)* Come to bed, my darling. My little darling is asleep. Come. . . . *(They go toward the door. In the distance a shepherd is playing his pipe.* TROFIMOV, *crosses the stage. When he sees* ANYA *and* VARYA *he stops*. Shhhhhh. She's asleep, asleep. Come on, darling.

ANYA *(speaking softly, half-asleep)*: I'm so tired. All those bells . . . tinkling . . . tinkling . . . Uncle, and Mamma, and Uncle . . .

VARYA: Come, little one. Come, darling. *(They go into* ANYA's *room.)* Come, my precious . . . angel . . . come.

TROFIMOV *(very moved)*: My own sunshine! My spring!

Act II

A meadow: an old, abandoned chapel, falling over; next to it a well and some large stones which were probably once tombstones, and an old bench. We see the road which leads to GAYEV'S *house. To one side are several dark poplar trees, and there starts the cherry orchard. Farther there is a row of telegraph poles. In the farthest distance one can guess the outline of a large town, visible only on very clear days. The sun will soon set.*

CHARLOTTA, YASHA, *and* DUNYASHA *are seated on the bench.* YEPIKHODOV *is standing playing the guitar. All look pensive.* CHARLOTTA, *who is wearing an old soldier's cap, has taken a shotgun from her shoulder and is adjusting the buckle on the strap.*

CHARLOTTA (*musingly*): I don't have a real passport; I don't even know my age, although I always feel like a little girl. When I was a child my father and mother traveled from one fair to another; they gave performances, very good performances too. And I did death-defying leaps, and things like that. Then, when Poppa and Mamma died, a German lady took me in and raised me. So that's how I grew up. Then I became a governess. But where do I come from, and who am I? I don't know a thing. Who were my parents? Were they even married? Who knows? *(She takes a cucumber from her pocket and munches it.)* I want so much to talk to someone. But who? There's nobody.

YEPIKHODOV *(playing the guitar and singing)*: "What care I for the noisy world? What is friend or foe to me?" How pleasant it is to play the mandolin.

DUNYASHA: That's a guitar, not a mandolin. *(She looks at herself in a little mirror and powders her face.)*

YEPIKHODOV: To a fool dying of love, this is a mandolin. *(Continuing to sing, softly)* "If only my lonely heart were warmed by the flame of love requited." *(YASHA sings softly with him.)*

CHARLOTTA: They sing dreadfully, these people. Faugh. Like jackals.

DUNYASHA *(to YASHA)*: How lucky you are to have been abroad.

YASHA: Yes, of course. I don't disagree. *(He yawns, then lights a cigar.)*

YEPIKHODOV: Yes, abroad everything has obviously reached completion.

YASHA: Of course.

YEPIKHODOV: I am a man of culture. I read all kinds of remarkable books. But the trouble is I do not manage to grasp the sense of my own thoughts. What is it that I wish, in fact: to live or to blow my brains out? Thus, I always carry a revolver. And here it is. *(He shows the revolver.)*

CHARLOTTA *(slinging the gun back over her shoulder)*: I'm finished now. I'm going. You're an intelligent man, Yepikhodov; you're dangerous. Women must be crazy about you. Brrr. *(She starts to go.)* Clever people are so stupid. I have no one to talk to. Alone, alone, I'm always alone. I have no one. . . . And who am I, why am I here? Nobody knows. *(She leaves unhurriedly.)*

YEPIKHODOV: Truth to tell, and putting all else aside, I must admit, in my own case, that fate treats me without pity: I am but a small ship tossed by the waves, and if this is not so, then I ask, for example, why, upon awakening this morning, did I perceive an enormous spider upon my chest . . . as big as this? *(He demonstrates with two hands.)* And, likewise, if I pick up a glass of *kvass*, why do I invariably find something indecent in it, like a cockroach? *(Pause.)* Have you read Buckle's *History of Civilization?* *(Pause.)* I would like a couple of words with you, Avdotya Fyodorovna, if you don't mind.

DUNYASHA: Well?

YEPIKHODOV: In fact . . . I would like to see you in private. *(Sighs.)*

DUNYASHA *(embarrassed):* Well . . . but first bring me my little cape. You'll find it near the cupboard. . . . It's rather damp out here.

YEPIKHODOV: Very well, Madame, I'll fetch it. Now I know what to do with my revolver. *(He takes his guitar and goes out playing it softly.)*

YASHA: Twenty-two misfortunes! Between you and me, he's stupid. . . . *(He yawns.)*

DUNYASHA: Still, I hope to God he doesn't shoot himself. *(Pause.)* I've become such a sensitive person. Everything upsets me now. I was a little girl when they took me to work in the master's house, and I've lost the habit of ordinary living. Look at my hands: they're white, white as a lady's. I've become so delicate, so sensitive, so ladylike. Everything frightens me. I'm scared. And if you deceive me, Yasha, what will happen to my nerves?

YASHA *(kissing her):* You little tomato. Young ladies don't lose their heads. I hate a girl who doesn't know how to conduct herself.

DUNYASHA: I love you passionately, Yasha. You're so educated. You can talk about anything. *(Pause.)*

YASHA *(yawning):* Mmmm . . . the way I see it, if a girl says she's in love, she's not a lady. *(Pause.)* I like smoking a cigar out here in the open air. *(He listens.)* They're coming . . . it's them. (DUNYASHA *kisses him effusively.)* Go home. Pretend you're coming from swimming in the river; take that path or they'll meet you and think I planned a rendezvous with you. I can't stand that sort of thing.

DUNYASHA *(with a little cough):* My head is aching from that cigar. *(She goes out.)*

> YASHA *remains sitting by the chapel.* LYUBOV AN-
> DREYEVNA, GAYEV, *and* LOPAKHIN *come in.*

LOPAKHIN: You must decide once and for all. Time won't wait. Just tell me: do you or don't you want to lease the land for summer cottages? Yes or no—just a word.

LYUBOV ANDREYEVNA: Who's been smoking those disgusting cigars out here? *(She sits down.)*

GAYEV: It's convenient now that the railroad is so near. Imagine: we had lunch in town. Cannon off the white! I'd like to go back to the house and play a game.

LYUBOV ANDREYEVNA: There'll be time enough for that.

LOPAKHIN: Just one word. *(Imploring)* Yes or no! Please tell me.

GAYEV *(yawning):* What?

LYUBOV ANDREYEVNA *(looking into her purse):* Yesterday there was lots of money in my purse. Today there's almost none. My poor Varya tries to save by feeding us only milk soup, and the old servants in the kitchen get nothing but dried peas while I just waste, I waste money. I don't know why. *(She drops her purse. Gold pieces fall. She's vexed.)* Now look. There they go.

YASHA: Permit me, Madame. I'll pick them up. *(He picks up the gold pieces.)*

LYUBOV ANDREYEVNA: Thank you, Yasha. Why did I go out to lunch with you, Leonya? That ugly restaurant of yours, that stupid music, and the tablecloths smelling of soap. . . . Why do you drink so much, Leonya? And eat so much? And talk so much? And to whom? To the waiters. Talking to the waiters, about the seventies and decadent literature—to the waiters!

LOPAKHIN: Unbelievable.

GAYEV *(with a gesture of resignation)*: I know. I know. I'm hopeless. That's obvious. *(Irritably to YASHA)* Why are you always hanging around, always bothering us?

YASHA *(laughing)*: Whenever I hear you talk I start to laugh. I always do. I can't help it.

GAYEV *(to his sister)*: Either he goes, or I go.

LYUBOV ANDREYEVNA: Go now, Yasha. *Allez vite!*

YASHA *(handing the purse back to* LYUBOV ANDREYEVNA*)*: Right away. I'm going. *(Hardly able to repress his laughter)* This minute. *(He goes out.)*

LOPAKHIN: They say Deriganov, the rich man, wants to buy your estate. He's coming to the auction in person.

LYUBOV ANDREYEVNA: Where did you hear that?

LOPAKHIN: They're talking about it in town.

GAYEV: Our aunt in Jaroslavl promised to send something, but when and how much, nobody knows.

LOPAKHIN: A hundred thousand? Two hundred?

LYUBOV ANDREYEVNA: More like ten or fifteen, and we'll be thankful for that.

LOPAKHIN: Forgive me, but I have never in my life met such impractical people as you, my friends. You are so un-businesslike. I have told you as clearly and as simply as I can: your estate is about to be sold, but you don't seem to understand. . . .

LYUBOV ANDREYEVNA: Well, what can we do? What? Tell us.

LOPAKHIN: I tell you and I tell you. I tell you every day. The cherry orchard and the land have got to be leased for summer cottages, and it must be done now, as soon as possible. The auction is almost here. Try and understand. Once you decide to allow the summer cottages to be built you'll have all the money you want. And you'll be saved.

LYUBOV ANDREYEVNA: All those little houses and those summer people. Forgive me, but it's so vulgar.

GAYEV: I couldn't agree with you more.

LOPAKHIN: I think I'm going to scream or faint or burst into tears! I can't stand it any more. You've worn me out! *(To GAYEV)* You're a silly old woman.

GAYEV: What?

LOPAKHIN: Silly old woman. *(He starts to leave.)*

LYUBOV ANDREYEVNA *(alarmed)*: No, dear friend. Stay, I beg you. We'll find a way.

LOPAKHIN: There is only one way.

LYUBOV ANDREYEVNA: Don't leave. I beg you. With you here somehow it seems more cheerful. . . . *(Pause.)* I keep feeling something awful is about to happen, as if the walls of the house were about to fall down on us.

GAYEV (*deep in thought*): Cannon off the middle. Pot the white.

LYUBOV ANDREYEVNA: We've sinned so much. . . .

LOPAKHIN: How have you sinned?

GAYEV (*putting a candy into his mouth*): They say I ate up my fortune in bon-bons. (*He laughs.*)

LYUBOV ANDREYEVNA: Oh, my sins . . . how I've sinned. . . . I've always been reckless with money, thrown it away like a lunatic, and I married a man who had a genius for debt. He died of champagne, my husband, he was always drunk. . . . And then, oh Lord, I fell in love with another man, I lived with him . . . and just at that time . . . it came, my first punishment . . . like a blow on the head! . . . My darling little Grisha, my beautiful boy, was drowned, here, right here, in this river. . . . I went away. I shut my eyes. I wanted never to come back, never to see the river again. I didn't want to know where I was, or what I was doing. I went abroad. But naturally *he* followed me, he wouldn't leave me alone. He was merciless, brutal. I bought a villa near Menton because he fell ill there. I had to nurse him. I had no rest for three years, day or night. He exhausted me, dried up my soul. Then last year when I had to sell the villa to pay our debts, we went to Paris, and there he robbed me and went to live with another woman. . . . I tried to poison myself, so stupid, so humiliating . . . and suddenly I felt such a longing, for Russia, for my own country, and for my little girl. . . . (*She wipes away her tears.*) God, God, be merciful, forgive my sins. Don't punish me any more. (*She takes a telegram from her pocket.*) I got this today from Paris—he begs me to forgive him and to come back. (*She tears up the telegram.*) Where's that music coming from? . . . (*She listens.*)

GAYEV: Our famous Jewish orchestra, do you remember? Four violins, a flute, and a double bass.

LYUBOV ANDREYEVNA: Does it still exist? We should have them come one night, give a party.

LOPAKHIN *(listening)*: I don't hear it. . . . *(He sings softly.)* "And the Germans if you pay, will turn the Russians into French so they say. . . ." *(He laughs.)* I saw a good play at the theater last night. It was very funny.

LYUBOV ANDREYEVNA: It probably wasn't funny at all. You shouldn't go to plays; you should look at yourselves instead. How grey your lives are, what useless things you say.

LOPAKHIN: That's true. I admit it frankly: our lives are stupid. *(Pause.)* My father was a peasant, an idiot. He knew nothing, and he taught me nothing. The only thing he ever did was beat me with a stick when he was drunk, and at bottom I'm a fool, exactly like him, the same sort of idiot. I never learned anything. I have a bad handwriting: I write like a pig. I'm ashamed to let people see it.

LYUBOV ANDREYEVNA: What? You need a wife, my friend.

LOPAKHIN: Yes . . . that's true.

LYUBOV ANDREYEVNA: Marry our Varya. She's a good girl.

LOPAKHIN: Yes.

LYUBOV ANDREYEVNA: She came to me from simple people, you know. Her family were peasants too, and she's a hard worker, but the main thing is, she loves you. And you've been fond of her for a long time.

LOPAKHIN: Well, why not? I have nothing against it. She's a good girl. *(Pause.)*

GAYEV: They've asked me to work at the bank, have you heard? Six thousand a year.

LYUBOV ANDREYEVNA: You? In a bank? Don't be ridiculous.

FIRS *enters, carrying a coat.*

FIRS *(to* GAYEV*):* Put this on, Sir. It's damp.

GAYEV *(putting on his coat):* You're such an old nuisance.

FIRS: Tsk . . . tsk . . . Never mind—You went off without even telling me this morning. *(He looks* GAYEV *over carefully.)*

LYUBOV ANDREYEVNA: How old you've become, Firs!

FIRS: What can I get you, Madame?

LOPAKHIN: She says: *you're very old.*

FIRS: I've lived a long time. They were looking for a wife for me before your Poppa was even born. *(He laughs.)* At the time the slaves were freed, I was already the head footman. I didn't want to be freed, and I stayed with the masters. . . . *(Pause.)* I remember everybody was happy then. Why? I don't know; they didn't know themselves.

LOPAKHIN: Oh, the old days were fine. . . . They could at least flog the peasants then.

FIRS *(not having heard):* That's right. The peasants took care of the masters, and the masters took care of the peasants, and they stuck together. Now everyone goes his own way, and who can understand anything?

GAYEV: Be quiet, Firs. Tomorrow I have to go to town. They promised to introduce me to a certain general who might give us a loan.

LOPAKHIN: Nothing will come of that, and besides I can tell you, you couldn't even pay the interest.

LYUBOV ANDREYEVNA: He's just talking nonsense. There is no such general, and there never has been.

TROFIMOV, ANYA, *and* VARYA *enter.*

GAYEV: Here come our little girls.

ANYA: There's Mamma!

LYUBOV ANDREYEVNA *(tenderly)*: Come, come here my darlings. *(She kisses* ANYA *and* VARYA.*)* If you only knew how I love you both. Sit here beside me—like this. *(They all sit.)*

LOPAKHIN: Our eternal student is always with the young ladies.

TROFIMOV: That's none of your business.

LOPAKHIN: Almost fifty and still a student.

TROFIMOV: Stop your stupid jokes.

LOPAKHIN: Why are you getting so angry, you strange man?

TROFIMOV: Leave me alone.

LOPAKHIN: Just let me ask you one question: what's your opinion of me?

TROFIMOV: This is my opinion, Yermolay Alexeyevich: you're a rich man. Soon you'll be a millionaire, and just as a beast of prey which devours everything in its path is necessary to the balance of nature, so you are necessary too. *(Everyone laughs.)*

VARYA: Tell us about the planets instead, Petya.

LYUBOV ANDREYEVNA: No, let's go on with yesterday's conversation.

TROFIMOV: What were we talking about?

GAYEV: Pride. Whether Man should be proud.

TROFIMOV: Yes, and we came to no conclusions. When you say Man should have pride in himself, you may be right, from a spiritual point of view. But if we take the question simply, and we don't try to complicate it: what is man that we should be so proud? Physiologically, he is pretty poorly constructed, and, in the vast majority of cases, he is vulgar, ignorant, and profoundly miserable. So why should we admire ourselves so much? The only thing to do is to work.

GAYEV: Why work? We're going to die anyway, whatever we do.

TROFIMOV: Who knows? And what does that mean: to die? Maybe Man has a hundred senses. Maybe only the five we know are going to die. Maybe the ninety-five others will go on living.

LYUBOV ANDREYEVNA: Petya, you're so clever.

LOPAKHIN (ironically): Frightening. . . !

TROFIMOV: Humanity is constantly advancing, trying to perfect itself. Everything that's unattainable now will one day be familiar, but we have to work at it. We must help those who are looking for the truth, but so far here in Russia few of us do any good work. The majority of our intellectuals look for no truths, and do nothing. They don't know how to work. They call themselves "the intelligentsia," but they treat their servants with contempt, and the peasants like animals. They don't know how to educate themselves. They don't read serious books; they don't do a thing except talk about science and pretend to understand art. They go around with grim faces discussing important thises and thats, philosophizing, while everyone can see that our workers are badly nourished, sleeping without proper beds, thirty or forty to a room, with bedbugs, foul odors, dampness, and immorality. Clearly all our fine talk serves only to divert and blind us. Show me where the public nurseries are that everyone is talking about. Show me the public libraries. You'll find them only in novels; in actuality, they don't exist. What does exist is filth, vulgarity, and our old Asian ways. I don't trust grave faces. They frighten me. And I mistrust serious conversations. We would do better to keep silent.

LOPAKHIN: Well, I can tell you, my friend, I get up at five in the morning, and work until night. I handle a lot of money, mine and others'; I get to see what people are like. You only have to start doing something to understand how few decent and honest people there are in this world. Sometimes when I can't sleep, I say to myself: Lord, you gave us these vast forests, these endless fields, these wide horizons; and we who live here ought to be giants.

LYUBOV ANDREYEVNA: Oh, dear, you want giants now. Why giants? They're all very well in fairy tales, but in real life they're rather alarming.

YEPIKHODOV *is passing in the background playing his guitar.*

LYUBOV ANDREYEVNA *(speaks dreamily)*: There goes Yepikhodov. . . .

ANYA *(dreamily)*: There goes Yepikhodov. . . .

GAYEV: Ladies and gentlemen, the sun has set.

TROFIMOV: Yes.

GAYEV *(quietly, as if reciting)*: Oh, glorious Nature, Wonderful, gleaming with eternal light, Beautiful and Indifferent, we call you our mother. You are our life, you are our death, you give us birth, and you destroy us. . . .

VARYA *(imploringly)*: Uncle, *please!*

ANYA: Uncle, you're doing it again.

TROFIMOV: You'd better bank the yellow in the middle pocket.

GAYEV: I'm silent, I'm silent.

All sit silently, deep in thought. FIRS *is muttering softly to himself. Suddenly a distant sound is heard, as if from the sky, like a snapped string, dying away, mournful.*

LYUBOV ANDREYEVNA: What was that?

LOPAKHIN: I don't know. Somewhere in a mine shaft, far away, a cable broke probably, and a bucket fell. But far away.

GAYEV: Or it might have been some bird—a heron. . . .

TROFIMOV: Or an owl.

LYUBOV ANDREYEVNA *(shivering)*: It was eerie. *(Pause.)*

FIRS: It was the same before the disaster: the owl hooted, the samovar sang without stopping, both.

GAYEV: Before what disaster?

FIRS: Before the emancipation. *(Pause.)*

LYUBOV ANDREYEVNA: Let's go, my friends. It's getting dark. *(To* ANYA*)* You have tears in your eyes—what is it, my little one? *(She holds her in her arms.)*

ANYA: Nothing, Mamma. Nothing.

TROFIMOV: Someone's coming.

A VAGRANT *appears in a shabby white soldier's cap and an overcoat; he's slightly drunk.*

VAGRANT: Excuse me. Sorry to disturb you. But tell me, can I get to the station this way?

GAYEV: You can. By that road.

VAGRANT: I thank you very much, Sir. *(He coughs.)* Beautiful weather we're having. *(He recites)* "Brother, oh suffering brother—come to the Volga." *(To* VARYA*)* Mademoiselle, will you give a hungry Russian thirty kopeks?

VARYA, *frightened, cries out.*

LOPAKHIN *(angrily)*: Really, that's enough.

LYUBOV ANDREYEVNA *(frightened, hurriedly)*: Here, this is for you. *(She searches frantically in her purse.)* No silver. It doesn't matter. Take a gold piece.

VAGRANT: Thank you very much, Madame. Much obliged to you, Madame. *(He goes out. Laughter.)*

VARYA *(frightened)*: I'm going . . . I'm going. Oh, Mamma, my poor Mamma. There's nothing in the house for the servants to eat, and you give him gold.

LYUBOV ANDREYEVNA: What's to be done with me? I'm so silly. When we get home I'll give you all I have in the house. Yermolay Alexeyevich, you'll lend me some more, won't you?

LOPAKHIN: Yes, Madame. Of course.

LYUBOV ANDREYEVNA: Come along everyone. It's time to go in. And just now, Varya, we've arranged a match for you. We've settled your marriage plans. Congratulations.

VARYA *(almost crying)*: Mamma, don't joke about that.

LOPAKHIN: "Get thee to a nunnery, Amelia."

GAYEV: Look, my hands are trembling; it's too long since I played billiards.

LOPAKHIN: "Amelia, O nymph, in thy horizons, be all my sins remembered."

LYUBOV ANDREYEVNA: Let's go, my friends! It's almost suppertime.

VARYA: He frightened me. My heart is pounding.

LOPAKHIN: Ladies and gentlemen, allow me to remind you: on the twenty-second of August the cherry orchard will be sold. Bear that in mind. Think. . . .

They all go out, except TROFIMOV *and* ANYA.

ANYA *(laughing)*: Thank you, stranger. He frightened Varya; and now we're alone.

TROFIMOV: Varya's afraid we'll fall in love; that's why all day long she won't leave us alone. She can't get it into her narrow mind that we're above love. To avoid the petty and illusory, that which prevents us from being free and happy, is the goal and meaning of our life. Forward! We march on irresistibly toward the bright star burning there in the distance. Forward! Don't fall behind, comrades!

ANYA *(extending her arms upward)*: How wonderfully you talk! *(Pause.)* It's so beautiful out today.

TROFIMOV: Yes, the weather's glorious.

ANYA: What have you done to me, Petya? Why don't I love the cherry orchard the way I used to? I loved it so much; it seemed to me there wasn't a better place in the world than our orchard.

TROFIMOV: All of Russia is our orchard. The world is vast and beautiful, and there are many wonderful places in it. *(Pause.)* Think, Anya: your grandfather, your great-grandfather, all your ancestors owned slaves, living souls. Can you hear their voices? Don't you feel human beings looking at you from every tree in the orchard? To have owned human souls has perverted you all—your ancestors and you who are alive now, so that your mother, your uncle, and even you don't realize it, but you're living in debt, at the expense of those who were your slaves. . . . We're behind by at least two hundred years. We've learned nothing yet, we're not even capable of judging our past. We only philosophize, complain, and drink vodka. But it's clear that to live in the present we must first redeem the past, atone for it, and that's only possible by suffering and by unceasing work. Understand that, Anya?

ANYA: The house we live in hasn't really been ours for a long time, and I'm going to leave it. I swear I will.

TROFIMOV: If you have the keys to the house, throw them into the well and leave. Be as free as the wind.

ANYA *(ecstatic)*: How well you said that!

TROFIMOV: Believe me, Anya, believe me, I'm not yet thirty, I'm still young and I'm still a student, but I have already seen so much. Every winter I'm hungry, sick, anxious, and poor as a beggar. Where hasn't Fate driven me? Where haven't I been, and yet, always, at every moment, my soul has been filled with incredible hope. I feel happiness coming, Anya, I can already see it. . . .

ANYA *(thoughtfully)*: The moon is rising.

YEPIKHODOV *is heard playing the guitar, the same sad song. The moon has risen. Somewhere behind the poplars* VARYA *is looking for* ANYA.

VARYA *(offstage, calling)*: Anya! Where are you?

TROFIMOV: Yes, the moon is rising. *(Pause.)* Happiness is here. It's coming closer. I hear its footsteps, and even if we don't see it, even if we don't know it, what does that matter? Others will see it after us!

VARYA *(offstage)*: Anya! Where are you?

TROFIMOV: Varya again. *(Angrily)* It's awful.

ANYA: Never mind her. Let's go down to the river. It's lovely there.

TROFIMOV: Yes, let's go. *(They go.)*

VARYA *(still offstage)*: Anya! Anya!

Act III

A drawing room separated from the ballroom by an arch. A chandelier is burning. From the hall we can hear the Jewish orchestra playing, the orchestra that was mentioned in Act II. Evening. In the ballroom they're dancing a Grand Rond.

SIMEONOV-PISHCHIK (*offstage*): *Promenade à une paire.*

> *The following couples enter the drawing room:* PISHCHIK *and* CHARLOTTA IVANOVNA, TROFIMOV *and* LYUBOV ANDREYEVNA, ANYA *and the* POST OFFICE CLERK, VARYA *with the* STATION MASTER, *and* DUNYASHA *and her partner, forming the last couple. As she dances,* VARYA *is crying quietly and wiping away her tears. They all go through the drawing room.*

PISHCHIK (*shouting*): *Grand rond, balancez! Les cavaliers à genoux et remerciez vos dames!*

> FIRS *in a frock coat carries a tray of seltzer water.* PISHCHIK *and* TROFIMOV *enter the drawing room.*

PISHCHIK: I'm an active man. I've had two strokes already and it's not good for me to dance. But, "If you want to run with the pack," as they say, "whether you bark or not, you should at least wag your tail." Anyway, I'm strong as a horse. My dear departed father—God rest his soul—maintained that the line of Simeonov-Pishchik descends from that horse which Caligula made a senator. . . . *(He sits down.)* I have only one trouble: money. Money. And, a hungry dog can only think of meat. *(He goes to sleep and snores, but immediately wakes up.)* Just like me . . . I can only talk about money.

TROFIMOV: It's true, now that you say it, there is something a little equine about you.

PISHCHIK: Well . . . the horse is not a bad animal . . . you can always sell it at least. . .

> *From the next room we hear the sound of billiard balls clicking against each other.* VARYA *appears under the arch.*

TROFIMOV *(teasing her)*: Madame Lopakhina! Madame Lopakhina!

VARYA *(angrily)*: Moth-eaten shabby old student!

TROFIMOV: Yes, moth-eaten, shabby, an old student and proud of it.

VARYA *(brooding bitterly)*: So now we've hired musicians, and how are we going to pay for them? *(She goes out.)*

TROFIMOV *(to* PISHCHIK*)*: If the energy you'd spent during your life looking for money to pay the interest on your debts had been used for something else, you'd probably have turned the world upside down.

PISHCHIK: Nietzsche, the philosopher . . . the greatest, the most famous . . . that gigantic intellect said that Man has the right to counterfeit money.

TROFIMOV: You've read Nietzsche?

PISHCHIK: Well . . . Dashenka mentioned him. . . . At the point I'm at, counterfeiting is the only thing left . . . day after tomorrow I owe three hundred ten roubles . . . I've already found a hundred. *(He feels his pockets, alarmed.)* The money's gone. I've lost it. *(Close to tears)* Where's the money? *(Joyously)* I have it; it's in the lining . . . I'm sweating. . . .

Enter LYUBOV ANDREYEVNA *and* CHARLOTTA IVANOVNA.

LYUBOV ANDREYEVNA *(hums the* Lezghinka, *a dance)*: Why hasn't Leonid come back? What can he be doing this long in town? *(To* DUNYASHA*)* Dunyasha, offer some tea to the musicians.

TROFIMOV: There probably wasn't any auction.

LYUBOV ANDREYEVNA: This wasn't the night for an orchestra, and we gave a party at the wrong time . . . well, never mind. *(She sits down and hums quietly.)*

CHARLOTTA *(she hands a pack of cards to* PISHCHIK*)*: Here's a deck of cards. Think of a card.

PISHCHIK: I've thought of one.

CHARLOTTA: Now shuffle the deck. Very good. Now, give them to me, my dear Monsieur Pishchik. *Eins, zwei, drei!* Now look for it. It's in your coat pocket.

PISHCHIK *(pulling a card out of his pocket)*: The eight of spades. That's absolutely right. *(Amazed)* Just think.

CHARLOTTA *(holding out the deck of cards toward* TROFI-MOV*)*: Quickly, what's the top card?

TROFIMOV: What? The queen of spades.

CHARLOTTA: Correct. *(To* PISHCHIK*)* And you? What's the top card?

PISHCHIK: The ace of hearts.

CHARLOTTA: Correct! *(She claps her hands and the deck of cards disappears.)* What beautiful weather we're having today.

The mysterious voice of a woman, seeming to come from under the floor, answers her.

VOICE: The weather is splendid, Madame.

CHARLOTTA: You are my ideal. You are beautiful. *Mon bel idéal.*

VOICE: And I too admire you, Madame.

STATION MASTER *(applauding)*: Bravo! Well done, Madame Ventriloquist.

PISHCHIK *(surprised)*: Just think . . . enchanting Charlotta Ivanovna, I am simply in love with you. *Vraiment! Ma parole!*

CHARLOTTA: In love? *(She shrugs her shoulders.)* How can you possibly be in love? *Guter Mensch, aber schlecter Musicant!*

TROFIMOV *(clapping PISHCHIK on the shoulder)*: Good old horse!

CHARLOTTA: Attention please! One more trick. *(She takes a lap robe from a chair.)* Here's a beautiful lap robe. I want to sell it. *(Shaking it out)* Does someone want to buy it?

PISHCHIK *(amazed)*: Just think!

CHARLOTTA: *Eins, zwei, drei! (She lifts the lap robe quickly. Behind it is* ANYA *who does a little curtsy, runs to her mother, kisses her, and runs back into the ballroom. Everyone is delighted.)*

LYUBOV ANDREYEVNA *(applauding)*: Bravo, bravo!

CHARLOTTA: Once again! *Eins, zwei, drei! (She lifts the lap robe behind which is* VARYA, *who bows.)*

PISHCHIK: Just think!

CHARLOTTA: That's all. Finished. *(She runs out.)*

PISHCHIK *(running after her)*: Oh, you little rascal. . . . What a woman, what a woman. *(He goes out.)*

LYUBOV ANDREYEVNA: And Leonid still hasn't come. What's he doing in town so long? I don't understand it. Either the estate has been sold and it's all over, or there's been no auction at all. Why keep us in suspense?

VARYA *(wanting to comfort her)*: Uncle has bought it. I am sure of it.

TROFIMOV *(ironic)*: Oh, of course.

VARYA: Great-Aunt sent him a power of attorney so that he could buy it in her name. She did it for Anya. And God will help us, I know; Uncle will buy the property.

LYUBOV ANDREYEVNA: Our great-aunt from Jaroslavl sent only fifteen thousand roubles to buy the estate—in *her* name. It's not even enough to pay the interest. She doesn't trust us. *(She covers her face with her hands.)* My fate will be decided today. My fate. . . .

TROFIMOV *(teasing* VARYA*)*: Madame Lopakhina.

VARYA *(angrily)*: Eternal student! You've already been expelled from the university twice.

LYUBOV ANDREYEVNA: Why are you getting angry, Varya? He's teasing you about Lopakhin. So? Why don't you marry Lopakhin? He's a good man, interesting. Of course you don't have to marry him if you don't want to. No one's forcing you, darling.

VARYA: I'm seriously thinking about it, Mamma. I am. He's a good man and I like him.

LYUBOV ANDREYEVNA: Then marry him. What are you waiting for? I don't understand.

VARYA: But, Mamma dear. I can't propose to him myself. For two years now everybody's been talking to me about it. But he either says nothing, or he jokes. I know why. He's busy getting rich; he's involved with his work; he doesn't have time to think of me. If only I had money, not even much money, even a hundred roubles, I would leave everything and go away, the farther the better. I would enter a convent.

TROFIMOV: How saintly.

VARYA (*to* TROFIMOV): A student is supposed to be smart. (*In a soft tone, with tears in her voice*) How ugly you've become, Petya, how old you've grown. (*To* LYUBOV ANDREYEVNA, *no longer crying*) I can't do without work, Mamma. I must have something to do every minute.

YASHA *enters.*

YASHA (*barely able to suppress his laughter*): Yepikhodov has broken a billiard cue. (*He goes out.*)

VARYA: What's Yepikhodov doing here? Who told him he could play billiards? I don't understand these people. (*She goes out.*)

LYUBOV ANDREYEVNA: Don't tease her, Petya. You can see she has enough troubles. . . .

TROFIMOV: But why does she take on so much? Why does she meddle? She hasn't left Anya and me alone the whole summer. She's afraid we're going to fall in love. And what business is that of hers? Besides, there's no reason to worry. We're far removed from such trivialities. We're above love.

LYUBOV ANDREYEVNA: And I suppose I'm below love. *(Agitated)*
Why hasn't Leonid come back? All I want to know is has
the estate been sold, yes or no? It seems inconceivable
to me . . . I don't know what to think . . . I'm losing my
mind . . . I could scream . . . do stupid things. Save me,
Petya. Say something.

TROFIMOV: Does it really matter whether the estate is sold or
not? All that has been finished for a long time. You can't
turn back the clock. Stay calm, dear Lyubov Andreyevna.
Don't fool yourself. At least once in your life, face the
truth.

LYUBOV ANDREYEVNA: What truth? You, of course, can always
see what's true and what's not true, but I can't. I'm blind.
You know the answers to all the important questions, but,
my dear, that's because you are young; the questions
haven't hurt you yet. You haven't suffered yet. When you
look forward, you look boldly; you see nothing to be afraid
of. Your young eyes haven't yet discovered life. You're
stronger and more honest than we are, less superficial,
that's true. But stop and think; be generous, have pity on
us. Try to imagine: I was born here; my parents lived here,
my grandfather lived here. I love this house; my life makes
no sense without the cherry orchard, and if it has to be
sold, then sell me too, with the orchard. . . . *(She embraces* TROFIMOV *and kisses him on the forehead.)* Remember, Petya, my little boy drowned here. . . . *(Crying)*
You have a good kind soul, my dear, have pity on me, have
pity.

TROFIMOV: You know I sympathize with you with all my heart.

LYUBOV ANDREYEVNA: You should have said that differently,
quite differently. . . . *(She takes out her handkerchief. A
telegram falls.)* My heart is heavy today; you can't imagine
how heavy. It's noisy here. I'm trembling, my very soul is
quivering, but I don't dare go to my room. I'm afraid of
being alone, of the silence. Don't judge me too harshly

Petya. I love you as if you were my own, and I would gladly give you my Anya, I swear it, but you must study, my dear, and get your degree. You're so strange. You do nothing. You live by simply allowing Fate to fling you from place to place, don't you? Don't you? It's true what I say, isn't it? And you must do something about your beard too, make it grow properly. . . . *(She laughs.)* You're so funny!

TROFIMOV *(he picks up the telegram)*: I don't want to look handsome.

LYUBOV ANDREYEVNA: A telegram from Paris. I get one every day. . . . That wild man is sick again. Something's still wrong with him . . . he wants me to forgive him, to come back, and it's true: I should go to Paris, stay with him a little. You look disapproving, Petya, but what else can I do, my dear? He's sick and miserable and alone. Who will take care of him; who will stop him from being silly, give him his medicine? And then, why hide it? Why not say so? I love him. It's true. I love him, I love him. He's a stone around my neck, he'll drag me down, but I love him. My own millstone; I can't live without him. *(She presses* TROFIMOV's *hand.)* Don't think badly of me, Petya, don't say anything, don't speak.

TROFIMOV *(almost crying)*: Excuse my saying so, but he's robbed you.

LYUBOV ANDREYEVNA: No, no, no. You musn't say that. . . . *(She puts her hands over her ears.)*

TROFIMOV: He's a scoundrel. Obviously. You're the only one who doesn't see it. A scoundrel.

LYUBOV ANDREYEVNA *(angry, but controlling herself)*: You're twenty-six years old, or twenty-seven, but you still act like a schoolboy.

TROFIMOV: So?

LYUBOV ANDREYEVNA: At your age you ought to be a man. Why

don't you fall in love, try to understand what love means. Fall in love with someone yourself. *(Angrily)* Yes, yes, it's not that you're so pure; you're a prude, that's what it is—a little boy, smug and ridiculous.

TROFIMOV *(horrified)*: What is she saying?

LYUBOV ANDREYEVNA: "I'm above love." You're not above love. You're simply a nincompoop, as Firs would say. When I think that at your age you don't even have a mistress!

TROFIMOV *(horrified)*: This is horrible! What is she saying? *(He goes quickly toward the ballroom, his head in his hands.)* Horrible. . . . I can't stand it. I'm going. . . . *(He goes out, but returns immediately.)* All is over between us! *(He goes out toward the hall.)*

LYUBOV ANDREYEVNA *(shouting after him)*: Petya, wait. You're so funny. I was just joking! *(We hear someone running up the stairs in the hall, then rolling back with a crash. We hear* ANYA *and* VARYA *scream, but then immediately we hear them laugh.)* What happened?

ANYA *runs in laughing.*

ANYA: Petya fell down the stairs! *(She runs out.)*

LYUBOV ANDREYEVNA: He's so funny, Petya.

The STATION MASTER *stops in the middle of the ballroom and begins to recite "The Sinner" by Alexei Tolstoy.* The others listen to him, but after only a few lines a waltz is heard, and all start to dance again.* TROFIMOV, ANYA, VARYA, *and* LYUBOV ANDREYEVNA *return.*

*The Sinner by Alexei Tolstoy:

The crowd swirls in merriment and laughter,
Among them, draining her cup to the dregs,
The Magdalene sits—beautiful young courtesan;
Her rich attire, her shameless dress
Proclaim her sinful life. . . .

LYUBOV ANDREYEVNA: But Petya. . . . Darling, forgive me, I beg you. Come and dance. . . . *(She dances with* PETYA. ANYA *and* VARYA *dance.* FIRS *enters, putting his cane near the door.* YASHA *also comes into the drawing room and watches the dancers.)*

YASHA: What's the matter, Grandpa?

FIRS: I don't feel well. In the old days generals came here, and admirals, and barons to dance at the balls, and now who do we send for? The Post Office Clerk and the Station Master, and even they have to be begged. I'm feeling weak. The old master, the grandfather, whenever anybody felt sick would give us sealing wax. I've been taking sealing wax now every day for twenty years. Maybe that's why I'm still alive.

YASHA: You bother me, Grandpa. *(He yawns.)* Why don't you go off and die?

FIRS: You, you . . . nincompoop . . . good for nothing. . . *(He mutters.)*

> TROFIMOV *and* LYUBOV ANDREYEVNA *dance in the ball-room, then in the drawing room.*

LYUBOV ANDREYEVNA: *Merci* . . . I must sit. *(She sits.)* I'm tired. . . .

> *Enter* ANYA.

ANYA *(all excited)*: Just now in the kitchen a man said the cherry orchard has already been sold.

LYUBOV ANDREYEVNA: To whom?

ANYA: He didn't say. He's gone. *(She dances with* TROFIMOV *into the ballroom.)*

YASHA: It was just an old man gossiping, a stranger.

FIRS: And Leonid Andreyevich not home yet. Not arrived. He

wore his light-weight coat. He'll catch cold. . . . Ach, ung people. . . .

LYUBOV ANDREYEVNA: I think I'm dying. Yasha, go quickly and find out who it was sold to.

YASHA: But he left a long time ago, the old man. *(He laughs.)*

LYUBOV ANDREYEVNA *(annoyed)*: What's so funny about that? What's so amusing?

YASHA *(laughs)*: That Yepikhodov. So stupid. There's no sense in him. Twenty-two disasters.

LYUBOV ANDREYEVNA: Firs, if the estate is sold, where will you go?

FIRS: Wherever you say.

LYUBOV ANDREYEVNA: Why do you look like that? Are you sick? You should go to bed. . . .

FIRS: Yes . . . *(With an ironic smile)* I will go to bed, and who will do the serving? Who'll keep order? There's only me for the whole house.

YASHA: Lyubov Andreyevna, may I ask you something please, a favor: if you go to Paris again, take me with you. It's impossible for me to remain here. *(He looks around him and lowers his voice.)* I don't need to tell you. You can see it for yourself. The country isn't civilized; the people have no morality, and besides, it's boring. The food in the kitchen is terrible, and there's that Firs always wandering around muttering. Please take me with you.

PISHCHIK *enters.*

PISHCHIK: May I have the pleasure of a little waltz, Most Bountiful Lady? (LYUBOV ANDREYEVNA *gets up to go with him.)* *Ma chère*, I still have to borrow those hundred and eighty roubles from you. . . . *(They dance.)* Just a hundred and eighty little roubles. *Un petit rien* . . . *(They dance into the ballroom.)*

YASHA *(singing softly)*: "Will you understand the torments of my heart?"

In the ballroom a figure in checked pants and a grey top hat waves both hands and jumps around. There are cries of "Bravo, Charlotta Ivanovna."

DUNYASHA *(stopping to powder her nose)*: The young mistress ordered me to dance; there are a lot of gentlemen and not enough ladies, but dancing makes my head spin. My heart is pounding. And, Firs Nikolayevitch, just now the Post Office Clerk said something to me so nice, oh, so nice that it took my breath away. *(The music plays more softly.)*

FIRS: What did he say?

DUNYASHA: You're like a flower, he said.

YASHA *(yawning)*: How stupid. *(He goes out.)*

DUNYASHA: Like a flower . . . I am so sensitive, so delicate; I love tender words. . . .

FIRS: That will be your undoing.

YEPIKHODOV *enters.*

YEPIKHODOV: You pay no more attention to me now, Avdotya Fyodorovna, than if I were an insect. *(He sighs.)* Ach, life.

DUNYASHA: But what can I do about it?

YEPIKHODOV: Undoubtedly, you may be right, of course. . . . *(He sighs.)* Still, if one considers it from another point of view, if I may so express myself, you've reduced me to an odd state, if, forgive my frankness, I may say so. And although I know my fate—each day a new disaster, I'm accustomed to it and I greet my life with a smile—still, you did give me your word and I'm——

DUNYASHA: Please, let's talk about it later. Right now, leave me alone. I'm in a dream. *(She plays with her fan.)*

YEPIKHODOV: Each day a new disaster, but, if I do say so myself, I merely smile; sometimes I even laugh.

VARYA *enters from the ballroom.*

VARYA: Haven't you gone yet, Semyon? You're so disrespectful. *(To* DUNYASHA*)* Dunyasha, leave us. *(To* YEPIKHODOV*)* First you play billiards and break a cue, and now you walk around the drawing room as if you were a guest.

YEPIKHODOV: You have no right to penalize me, if I may say so.

VARYA: I'm not penalizing you. I'm telling you. You do nothing but wander around from one room to another and you never do any work. I wonder why we employ a clerk at all.

YEPIKHODOV *(offended)*: Whether I work, or eat, or wander around, or play billiards, that is the concern of people of understanding. Only my elders may judge me.

VARYA: How dare you say that to me? *(Getting very angry)* How dare you? *I* don't understand anything? Get out of here! This very instant!

YEPIKHODOV *(alarmed)*: I beg you, express yourself more delicately.

VARYA *(beside herself)*: Get out! Clear out. Now. Out. Out! *(He goes toward the door; she follows him.)* Twenty-two misfortunes! Out. I don't want to see you here any more. Out! *(*YEPIKHODOV *goes out. We hear his voice from behind the door.)*

YEPIKHODOV *(offstage)*: I'm going to lodge a complaint against you.

VARYA: What! You're coming back? (*She grabs the cane forgotten by* FIRS.) All right, come back. I'll teach you. . . . You'll see. . . . Come on now, come in . . . this is for you. . . . (*She swings the cane at the moment that* LOPAKHIN *enters.*)

LOPAKHIN: Thank you.

VARYA (*angrily and ironically*): I beg your pardon. I hope you'll forgive me.

LOPAKHIN: Not at all. Thank you for your warm reception.

VARYA: Don't mention it. (*She moves off, then turns around and asks him gently*) Did I hurt you?

LOPAKHIN: No, it's nothing. There'll be a big bump.

Voices in the ballroom.

VOICES: Lopakhin is here. Lopakhin has come back. Lopakhin has arrived. Yermolay Alexeyevich.

PISHCHIK *enters.*

PISHCHIK: It's him. He's here. He's back. Look! He's actually here. You can see him! You can touch him! (*He kisses* LOPAKHIN.) You smell of brandy, dear heart. We've been having a good time too.

LYUBOV ANDREYEVNA *enters.*

LYUBOV ANDREYEVNA: Yermolay Alexeyevich. Where were you? Where's Leonid?

LOPAKHIN: Leonid Andreyevich came back with me He's coming. . . .

LYUBOV ANDREYEVNA (*agitated*): Well? What happened? Was there an auction? Say something Speak!

LOPAKHIN (*embarrassed, afraid of showing his joy*): The auction was over at four. . . . We missed the train and had to wait until 9:30. *(Sighing heavily)* Ugh, my head is spinning.

GAYEV *enters.*

LYUBOV ANDREYEVNA: What happened? Quick! Tell us, Leonya, for God's sake!

GAYEV *(gestures helplessly, not answering her. He speaks loudly to* FIRS*)*: Here, take these. There are some anchovies and herrings. I haven't eaten anything all day. Oh, what I've been through. . . .

> *The door of the billiard room is open; we hear the noise of billiard balls clicking and* YASHA's *voice.*

YASHA *(offstage)*: Seven and eighteen.

GAYEV *(his face changes; he stops crying)*: I'm tired. Come help me change, Firs. *(He goes to his room through the ballroom,* FIRS *following.)*

PISHCHIK: What about the auction? What happened? Tell us.

LYUBOV ANDREYEVNA: Is the cherry orchard sold?

LOPAKHIN: It's sold.

LYUBOV ANDREYEVNA: Who bought it?

LOPAKHIN: I bought it.

> *Pause.* LYUBOV ANDREYEVNA *is overcome; she would fall if she weren't near an armchair and table.* VARYA *undoes the ring of keys from her belt, throws it into the middle of the drawing room and goes out.)*

LOPAKHIN: Yes, I bought it. Wait, my friends, please. My head is spinning; I can't talk. *(He laughs.)* We got to the auction; Deriganov was already there. Leonid Andreyevich had only fifteen thousand roubles. First thing, Deriganov bids thirty thousand above and beyond the mortgage. I see what's happening. I jump in and bid forty thousand. He bids forty-five; I bid fifty-five. He goes up by five thousands; I go up by tens. In the end I bid ninety thousand roubles plus the mortgage, and I got it. Now the cherry orchard is mine. Mine! *(He bursts out laughing.)* Dear God, the cherry orchard is mine! It's mine. Tell me I'm drunk, tell me I'm crazy, I'm dreaming. *(He stamps his feet.)* Don't laugh at me. If only my father and my grandfather could rise from their graves and see me now: their ignorant little Yermolay who was beaten, who went without shoes in the winter, has bought the estate, the most beautiful estate in the world! I bought the estate where my father and my grandfather were slaves. They weren't even allowed into the kitchen. I must be dreaming, asleep, imagining. This only seems like it's happening. It can't be true! *(He picks up the keys and speaks with a gentle smile.)* She threw down her keys. It must be because she's not mistress here any more. *(He jingles the keys.)* Well, so it must be.

We hear the musicians tuning their instruments.

Hey, musicians, play, I want to hear you. I want music. Everyone come and look how Yermolay Alexeyevich is going to take an ax to the cherry orchard; the trees are going to fall! Yes, yes—we're going to build new houses, and our grandchildren and our great-grandchildren are going to live a new life here. . . . Play! Music!

The music plays. LYUBOV ANDREYEVNA *falls into a chair, crying bitterly.*

LOPAKHIN *(remorsefully)*: Why didn't you listen to me, my poor friend? Dear Lady, we can't undo it now. *(Through tears)* Oh, if only all this would be over soon . . . if only somehow our miserable unhappy lives could change.

PISHCHIK *(taking him by the arm, speaking in a low tone)*: She's crying. Let's go into the ballroom. Leave her alone. Come. . . . *(He takes* LOPAKHIN's *arm and leads him into the ballroom.)*

LOPAKHIN: What's the matter? Come on music, play louder! Let everything be the way *I* want it. *(Ironically)* Here comes the new master of the cherry orchard. *(He accidentally bumps into a small table and nearly knocks over some candlesticks.)* It's all right. I can pay for everything. *(He goes out with* PISHCHIK.*)*

There's no one left in the ballroom or the drawing room except LYUBOV ANDREYEVNA *who sits huddled up in a chair crying bitterly. The music plays quietly.* ANYA *and* TROFIMOV *enter quickly.* ANYA *goes to her mother and kneels in front of her.* TROFIMOV *remains standing in the entrance to the ballroom.*

ANYA: Mamma! Mamma, you're crying. My dear sweet Mamma . . . my beautiful Mamma. . . . I love you. Bless you. The cherry orchard is sold, no more cherry orchard, it's gone, that's true, it's true, but you mustn't cry, Mamma. You still have your life in front of you; you still have your own pure soul. Come with me now, come, my darling, let's leave here. We'll plant a new orchard, more beautiful than this one, you'll see, you'll understand, and joy, deep quiet joy, Mamma, you'll feel it in your heart, like a sunset and you'll smile, Mamma! Come, darling, come. . . .

Act IV

The scene is the same as Act I, but there are no curtains on the windows or pictures on the walls. What little furniture is left is piled up in one corner, as if for sale. There's a feeling of emptiness. Near the outside door, at the back of the stage, are suitcases, traveling bags, etc. The door on the left is open. From it are heard ANYA's *and* VARYA's *voices.* LOPAKHIN *is standing, waiting.* YASHA *holds a tray of champagne glasses. In the entrance hall* YEPIKHODOV *is tying a box with a string. From offstage there is the sound of people talking—peasants who have come to say goodbye. We hear* GAYEV's *voice speaking to them.*

GAYEV *(offstage):* Thank you, brothers, thank you.

YASHA: The peasants have come to say goodbye. In my opinion, Yermolay Alexeyevich, peasants are good people, but they don't know much.

The sound of the voices subsides. LYUBOV ANDREYEVNA *and* GAYEV *enter from the hall.* LYUBOV ANDREYEVNA *is not crying, but she's pale. Her face quivers. She's unable to speak.*

GAYEV: You gave them your purse, Lyuba. You musn't do things like that . . . you musn't. . . .

LYUBOV ANDREYEVNA: I couldn't help it. I couldn't help it. *(They go out.)*

LOPAKHIN *(at the door, calling after them)*: Please have some champagne before you go. I forgot to get some in town, but I found one bottle at the station. So please, have some. *(Pause.)* No? You don't want any? *(He comes back from the door.)* If I had known that, I wouldn't have bought it. Well, then I won't have any either. (YASHA *carefully puts the tray on a chair.)* You have some at least, Yasha.

YASHA: Good health to those who are leaving; good health to those who are staying. . . . *(He drinks.)* This isn't French champagne, I can assure you.

LOPAKHIN: Eight roubles a bottle. *(Pause).* It's colder than hell here.

YASHA: They didn't light the fire today, since we're all leaving. *(He laughs.)*

LOPAKHIN: What's so funny?

YASHA: Nothing. Just laughing for joy.

LOPAKHIN: Here it is October, but it's sunny out, and there's no wind; it's like summer. Good for building. *(He looks at his watch and calls toward the door.)* Ladies and gentlemen, keep in mind: your train leaves in forty-seven minutes. In twenty minutes you have to leave for the station. Better hurry up.

TROFIMOV *enters from outside in an overcoat.*

TROFIMOV: I think it's time to leave. The horses are ready. Where are my galoshes? They're lost. *(Calling through the door)* Anya, where are my galoshes? I can't find them.

LOPAKHIN: I have to go to Kharkov on the same train as you. I'm spending the winter in Kharkov. I've been wasting time here gossiping with you all, and I'm sick of doing nothing. I can't stand to be without work, don't know what to do with my hands. See how they're hanging. As if they didn't belong to me.

TROFIMOV: Well, we're leaving now so you can get back to your useful occupations.

LOPAKHIN: Have a glass of champagne.

TROFIMOV: No, I don't want any.

LOPAKHIN: So you're going to Moscow.

TROFIMOV: Yes. I accompany them to town, and tomorrow I go to Moscow.

LOPAKHIN: Yes. . . . Well, I suppose the professors are all waiting for you.

TROFIMOV: Mind your own business.

LOPAKHIN: How many years is it you've been studying at the university?

TROFIMOV: Try to think of something else. That joke is getting stale. *(He looks for his galoshes.)* Listen, we may never see each other again, so let me tell you something now; stop throwing your arms about, get rid of that habit of making grand sweeping gestures. Yes. And all this talk about building villas, believing that the summer residents are going to cultivate the land; that's a grand sweeping gesture too. . . . Still, in spite of everything, I like you, you know. . . . You have fine, sensitive fingers, artist's fingers, and a fine sensitive soul. . . .

LOPAKHIN *(embracing him)*: Goodbye, dear friend. Thank you for everything. Let me give you some money for the trip.

TROFIMOV: Why? I don't need it.

LOPAKHIN: But you don't have any.

TROFIMOV: Yes I have, thanks. I just got some for a translation. *(Anxious)* But I can't find my galoshes.

VARYA *(from the next room)*: Here are your filthy galoshes. *(She throws them to the middle of the stage.)*

TROFIMOV: What are you so angry about, Varya? And these aren't my galoshes.

LOPAKHIN: I planted three thousand acres of poppies this spring. And cleared a profit of forty thousand roubles. It was beautiful when the poppies were blooming, a beautiful picture. Anyway, I've made forty thousand so if I'm offering you a loan it's because I can afford to. Why turn up your nose? I'm a peasant; I speak straight out.

TROFIMOV: So your father was a peasant. Mine was a pharmacist. So? *(LOPAKHIN takes out his wallet.)* Put it away. You could give me two thousand and I wouldn't want it. I'm a free man. Money, which you rich men value so highly, and poor men too, has no power over me. It's just feathers in the wind. I don't need you, I can pass you by; I'm strong, I'm proud. Humanity is marching toward a higher truth, toward the greatest possible happiness on earth, and I'm in the front ranks.

LOPAKHIN: And will you get there?

TROFIMOV: I'll get there. *(Pause.)* I'll get there, or I'll show others how to get there.

> *From a distance we hear axes striking the trunks of trees.*

LOPAKHIN: Well, dear friend, goodbye. Time to go. We play at being proud; we show off to each other while life goes on, paying no attention to us. When I've worked for a long time without stopping then my thoughts are lighter, and it seems to me that I also know why I'm alive. But how many of us in Russia, brother, know why we exist? Well, never mind. It doesn't matter. That's not what pays the rent. It seems Leonid Andreyevich has accepted a position in a bank, six thousand a year . . . he won't last long there; he's too lazy.

ANYA *(at the door)*: Mamma asks that you not cut down the trees before she goes.

TROFIMOV: That's true. You really might have had the tact. . . . *(He goes out through the hall.)*

LOPAKHIN: Of course, of course . . . these workers, really. . . . *(He follows* TROFIMOV *out.)*

ANYA: Did they take Firs to the hospital?

YASHA: I told them to this morning. One assumes that they did.

ANYA *(to* YEPIKHODOV*)*: Semyon Panteleyevich, please ask if Firs has been taken to the hospital.

YASHA *(offended)*: I told Egor this morning. Why ask ten times?

YEPIKHODOV: The venerable Firs, in my opinion, has already lived too long; he's past mending; he should join his ancestors. And I can only envy him. *(He puts a suitcase on a hat box which he crushes.)* There. Naturally. I knew it. *(He goes out.)*

YASHA *(making fun of him)*: Twenty-two disasters!

VARYA *(from behind the door)*: Did they take Firs to the hospital?

ANYA: Yes.

VARYA: Then why didn't they take the letter for the doctor?

ANYA *(as she goes out)*: We'll have to send it right away.

VARYA *(from behind the door)*: Where's Yasha? Tell him his mother's here. She wants to say goodbye.

YASHA *(with a gesture of annoyance)*: So exasperating. . . .

DUNYASHA, *who has been busy with the baggage, goes up to* YASHA *as soon as they're alone.*

DUNYASHA: You might look at me at least once, Yasha. You're leaving, you're abandoning me. . . . *(She throws herself on his neck, crying.)*

YASHA: What's the good of crying? *(He drinks some champagne.)* In six days: Paris! Tomorrow we take the express, and poof: we're gone. You'll never see us again. I can hardly believe it. *Vive la France!* I don't feel good here. I can't get used to it. . . . There's nothing to do all day, and I'm sick of all this ignorance: I've had enough of it. *(He drinks some champagne.)* What's the use of crying? If you were a girl who behaved properly, you wouldn't find yourself crying.

DUNYASHA *(powdering her nose and looking into her small pocket mirror)*: Write to me. I've loved you so much, Yasha. So much! I'm a delicate sensitive creature. I have too soft a heart.

YASHA: They're coming. *(He busies himself with the baggage, humming.)*

ـYUBOV ANDREYEVNA, GAYEV, ANYA, *and* CHARLOTTA IVANOVNA *enter.*

GAYEV: We ought to go. It's almost time. *(Looking at* YASHA*)* Who smells of herring in here?

LYUBOV ANDREYEVNA: In another ten minutes we'll have to get into the carriage. *(She looks around her.)* Goodbye, dear house, old ancestor . . . winter will pass, and spring will come, and you'll no longer be here . . . torn down. How much these walls have seen. *(She kisses her daughter warmly.)* My little treasure, you're beaming. Your eyes are like two diamonds. Are you happy? Very happy?

ANYA: Yes, Mamma. I'm happy. A new life is starting.

GAYEV *(happily)*: So everything is all right now. Before the cherry orchard was sold we worried and we suffered. But now that everything's settled, we're calm, calm and happy . . . here I am a banker, a financier . . . yellow ball to the side pocket and you, Lyuba, look better. You do.

LYUBOV ANDREYEVNA: Yes. My nerves are calmer. That's true. . . . *(She is brought her coat and hat.)* I sleep better now. Take my things, Yasha. It's time. *(To* ANYA*)* My little girl. We'll see each other soon. I have to go back to Paris. I'll live there on the money your great-aunt sent us to buy back the estate. God Bless dear Auntie! But the money won't last long. . . .

ANYA: You'll come back soon, Mamma, soon . . . won't you? I'll study for my exams, and pass them, and then I'll go to work. I'll be able to help you. . . . We'll read lots of books together, Mamma . . . won't we? *(She kisses her mother's hands.)* In the autumn evenings, we'll read books . . . a wonderful new world will open for us. . . . *(Daydreaming)* You will come back, Mamma, won't you?

LYUBOV ANDREYEVNA: I'll come back, my precious treasure. *(She embraces her daughter.)*

LOPAKHIN *enters.* CHARLOTTA *quietly hums a little song.*

GAYEV: Lucky Charlotta; she's singing.

CHARLOTTA *(taking up a bundle that looks like a baby wrapped in swaddling clothes)*: Hush-a-bye, baby. *(We hear the baby crying: "Oh ah.")* Hush, hush, little baby, poor little baby, bye, bye, baby. . . . *("Oh ah, oh, ah")* I'm so sorry for you. You're breaking your Mama's heart. *(She throws the bundle down.)* Will you find me another job, please. I need one.

LOPAKHIN: We'll find you a job, Charlotta Ivanovna. Don't you worry. We'll find you a job.

GAYEV: Everyone's leaving. Varya's going away. . . . Suddenly no one needs us any more.

CHARLOTTA: There's no place for me to live in town. I have to go elsewhere. *(She hums.)* It doesn't matter anyway.

Enter PISHCHIK.

LOPAKHIN: Here's our miracle of nature!

PISHCHIK *(out of breath, panting)*: Ouf . . . Let me catch my breath . . . I'm exhausted . . . I salute you all . . . give me some water. . . .

GAYEV: I suppose he's come for money again. Excuse me. Time to make myself scarce. *(He goes out.)*

PISHCHIK: I haven't been to see you for such a long time, Most Beautiful Lady. *(To* LOPAKHIN*)* And you're here too . . . good to see you, oh Great Genius. Here . . . take this . . . *(giving* LOPAKHIN *a bundle of bills)* four hundred roubles—I still owe you eight hundred forty. . . .

LOPAKHIN *(shrugging his shoulders, bewildered)*: I must be dreaming. Where did you get it?

PISHCHIK: Wait . . . I'm too warm . . . an extraordinary event! Some Englishmen came, discovered some white clay on my land. . . . *(To* LUYBOV ANDREYEVNA*)* Here's four hundred for you, Most Beautiful and Wonderful Lady. . . . *(He hands her the money.)* The rest will come later. *(He takes a drink of water.)* Just now, on the train, a young man was saying that a great philosopher wrote: "Everyone should dare to jump off the roof. Jump," he said, "and that'll settle everything." *(Amazed)* Just think! Water, please.

LOPAKHIN: What about the Englishmen?

PISHCHIK: I leased them the land with the white clay for twenty-four years . . . and now, excuse me, but I have to go . . . to the next place. I'm going to Znoikov's, then to Kardamanov's. . . . I owe everybody money. *(He drinks.)* Good health to you all. I'll come by again on Thursday.

LYUBOV ANDREYEVNA: We're moving to town today. Tomorrow I'm going abroad.

PISHCHIK: What! *(Alarmed)* To town? So that's it . . . furniture . . . suitcases . . . well, that's all right. *(Almost crying)* That's all right. . . . Remarkably intelligent, those Englishmen. . . . That's all right . . . be happy . . . God will help you . . . that's all right. Everything comes to an end in this world. . . . *(He kisses* LYUBOV ANDREYEVNA's *hand.)* And if one day you should hear that I'm dead, think of . . . Caligula's horse, and say: "Once upon a time there lived a certain Simeonov-Pishchik, may God rest his soul" . . . wonderful weather we're having . . . yes. . . . *(He goes out, obviously shaken, but returns immediately and speaks from the door.)* Dashenka sends her regards. *(He goes out.)*

LYUBOV ANDREYEVNA: Now we can leave, but I still have two worries. The first is Firs who is sick. *(She looks at her watch.)* We have five minutes.

ANYA: They took Firs to the hospital, Mamma. Yasha sent him this morning.

LYUBOV ANDREYEVNA: My second worry is Varya. She's so used to getting up early and working hard. And now, with nothing to do, she's like a fish out of water. She's gotten thin and pale; she cries all the time, poor dear. . . . *(Pause)*. You know as well as I do, Yermolay Alexeyevich, that I've always dreamed of her marrying you, and there's been every sign that you would marry her. *(She whispers to* ANYA *who nods to* CHARLOTTA, *and they both go out.)* She loves you: you're fond of her, and, I don't know . . . I don't understand why you seem to run away from each other.

LOPAKHIN: I don't understand it either, as a matter of fact. It's peculiar. . . . But if there's time, I'm still ready, right now even. . . . Let's finish this business once and for all because when you're gone I know I won't be able to ask her.

LYUBOV ANDREYEVNA: Good! After all, one minute is enough. I'll call her.

LOPAKHIN: We even have champagne here. *(He looks at the glasses.)* Empty. Someone's drunk it all. *(*YASHA *laughs.)* You might call that guzzling it down.

LYUBOV ANDREYEVNA *(animatedly)*: Good. Now we'll leave you two alone. Yasha, *allez!* I'll call her. *(Calling through the door)* Varya, come here a moment . . . alone. Come here! *(She goes out with* YASHA.*)*

LOPAKHIN *(looking at his watch)*: Yes. . . . *(Pause.)* *(From behind the door: stifled laughs, whispering, and finally* VARYA *enters.)*

VARYA *(carefully examining the baggage)*: That's funny. I can't find it anywhere.

LOPAKHIN: What are you looking for?

VARYA: I packed it myself, but I don't remember where. *(Pause.)*

LOPAKHIN: Where will you go now, Varvara Mikhalovna?

VARYA: Me? To the Ragoulines. I agreed I'd go there and look after the house . . . to be a housekeeper, or something. . . .

LOPAKHIN: At Yashnevo? That's about seventy miles from here. *(Pause.)* Well, life in this house seems to be over.

VARYA *(examining the baggage)*: Where did I put it? Unless it's in a trunk. . . . Yes, life in this house is over. . . . There won't be any more.

LOPAKHIN: And me, I'm off to Kharkov in a little while . . . taking the same train. I've got a lot to do. I'm leaving Yepikhodov here. I've hired him.

VARYA: Have you?

LOPAKHIN: Last year at this time it was already snowing, if you remember, and now it's quiet and sunny . . . but there's frost; it's three degrees out. . . .

VARYA: I haven't looked at the thermometer. *(Pause.)* Anyway, ours is broken. *(Pause.) (A voice from the courtyard is heard calling: "Yermolay Alexeyevich!")*

LOPAKHIN *(as if he'd been expecting this call for a long time)*: Coming! *(He goes out quickly.)*

> VARYA, *sitting on the floor, her head on a bundle, sobs softly. The door opens.* LYUBOV ANDREYEVNA *enters cautiously.*

LYUBOV ANDREYEVNA: Well? *(Pause.)* We have to go.

VARYA *(no longer crying, wipes her eyes)*: Yes, Mamma dear, it's time. I'll reach the Ragoulines today, if only we don't miss the train.

LYUBOV ANDREYEVNA *(calling in the direction of the door)*: Anya, put on your coat. (ANYA *enters, then* GAYEV *and* CHARLOTTA. GAYEV *wears a winter coat with a hood. The servants enter and the drivers.* YEPIKHODOV *fusses around the baggage.)* And now, we start our travels.

ANYA *(joyfully)*: On our way!

GAYEV: My friends, my dear good friends, now leaving this house forever, how can I be silent? How can I not express the profound feelings with which my whole being—

ANYA *(pleading)*: Uncle! . . .

VARYA: Uncle, dear, you musn't. . . .

GAYEV *(dejectedly)*: Double off the white . . . yellow to the side pocket. I'm silent.

TROFIMOV *enters, and then* LOPAKHIN.

TROFIMOV: Well, ladies and gentlemen, time to go.

LOPAKHIN: Yepikhodov, my coat!

LYUBOV ANDREYEVNA: Let me sit here just another minute. . . . It's as if I'd never seen the walls of this room before, or the ceiling. I'm looking at them so greedily now, with such love. . . .

GAYEV: I remember one day when I was six, right after Easter, I sat on the edge of this window watching my father going to church. . . .

LYUBOV ANDREYEVNA: Have they taken all the things out?

LOPAKHIN: I think so, yes. *(Putting on his coat, speaking to* YEPIKHODOV*)* You keep things in order here, Yepikhodov.

YEPIKHODOV *(with a hoarse voice)*: You have nothing to worry about, Yermolay Alexeyevich.

LOPAKHIN: What's the matter with your voice?

YEPIKHODOV: I drank some water a little while ago. I must have swallowed it wrong.

YASHA *(contemptuously)*: Such ignorance.

LYUBOV ANDREYEVNA: We're going, and not a soul will be living here any more. . . .

LOPAKHIN: Until the spring.

VARYA *(pulls out her umbrella, which was already in a parcel, with a sharp gesture as if she were going to hit someone with it.* LOPAKHIN *pretends to be frightened.)*: What's the matter with you? What's the matter with you? It didn't even occur to me.

TROFIMOV: My friends, to carriage! It's time. The train won't wait.

VARYA: Petya, here are your galoshes. They were behind this suitcase. *(Almost crying.)* They're so worn and dirty.

TROFIMOV *(putting on his rubbers)*: Let's go, my friends. Ladies and gentlemen, let's go.

GAYEV *(extremely troubled, afraid of crying)*: The train . . . the station. . . . Cross table to the center. Double the white into the corner.

LYUBOV ANDREYEVNA: Come, let's go!

LOPAKHIN: Is everyone here? Nobody's in there? *(He locks the door on the left.)* Have we left anything? Have to lock up. Let's go! . . .

ANYA: Goodbye, house! Goodbye, our old life.

TROFIMOV: Long live our new life.

> TROFIMOV *and* ANYA *go out.* VARYA *glances around once more and goes out unhurriedly.* YASHA, *and* CHARLOTTA *with her little dog, follow her.*

LOPAKHIN: Until spring. Come, friends . . . till we meet again. *(He goes out.)*

LYUBOV ANDREYEVNA *and* GAYEV *are left alone. As if they had been waiting for this moment they throw themselves into each other's arms and sob restrainedly, holding back, afraid of being heard.*

GAYEV *(in despair)*: My sister! My sister!

LYUBOV ANDREYEVNA: Oh, my orchard, my dear, sweet, beautiful orchard! My life, my youth, my happiness. Farewell.

ANYA's *voice is heard calling joyfully.*

ANYA *(offstage)*: Mamma!

TROFIMOV *(offstage, gay and animated)*: Auuu . . . Auuu . . .

LYUBOV ANDREYEVNA: One last look at these walls, at these windows . . . our dear mother; she loved to walk around this room.

GAYEV: My sister! My sister!

ANYA *(offstage)*: Mamma!

TROFIMOV *(offstage)*: Auuu . . . Auuu . . .

LYUBOV ANDREYEVNA: We're coming.

They go out. The stage is empty. We hear the doors being locked. The carriages leave. It becomes very quiet. There is only the muffled sound of an ax hitting a tree, a lonely and sad sound.

Some steps. FIRS *appears at the door on the right. He is dressed as usual in a frock coat, a white vest, and slippers. He is sick.*

FIRS *(going to the door, turning the handle)*: It's locked. They're gone. . . . *(He sits on the couch.)* They've forgotten me. It doesn't matter . . . I'll sit here for a while. I'm sure Leonid Andreyevich didn't put on his fur coat; he's gone out in his thin overcoat. *(He sighs anxiously.)* And I didn't watch him . . . ach, still like a child. . . . *(He mutters some words which we cannot understand.)* So life has gone by now . . . and it seems I still haven't lived. *(He lies down on the couch.)* I'm going to lie down for a while. You have no more strength, nothing left in you . . . nothing . . . ah, go on, you nincompoop . . . good for nothing. . . .

He remains lying down, not moving. In the distance, as if from the sky, there is the sound of a snapped string, a melancholy sound which dies away little by little. Then silence; we hear only the sound of the axes against the trees, far away in the orchard.

Selected List of Grove Press Drama and Theater Paperbacks

E449   ARDEN, JOHN / Armstrong's Last Goodnight / $1.50

E312   ARDEN, JOHN / Serjeant Musgrave's Dance / $2.45 [See also Modern British Drama, Henry Popkin, ed. GT614 / $5.95]

B109   ARDEN, JOHN / Three Plays: Live Like Pigs, The Waters of Babylon, The Happy Haven / $2.45

E610   ARRABAL, FERNANDO / And They Put Handcuffs on The Flowers / $1.95

E486   ARRABAL, FERNANDO / The Architect and The Emperor of Assyria / $2.40

E611   ARRABAL, FERNANDO / Garden of Delights / $2.95

E521   ARRABAL, FERNANDO / Guernica and Other Plays (The Labyrinth, The Tricycle, Picnic on the Battlefield) / $2.45

E532   ARTAUD, ANTONIN / The Cenci / $1.95

E127   ARTAUD, ANTONIN / The Theater and Its Double (Critical Study) / $2.95

E425   BARAKA, IMAMU AMIRI (LEROI JONES) / The Baptism and The Toilet / $2.45

E471   BECKETT, SAMUEL / Cascando and Other Short Dramatic Pieces (Words and Music, Film, Play, Come and Go, Eh Joe, Endgame) / $1.95

E96   BECKETT, SAMUEL / Endgame / $1.95

E318   BECKETT, SAMUEL / Happy Days / $2.45

E226   BECKETT, SAMUEL / Krapp's Last Tape, plus All That Fall, Embers, Act Without Words I and II / $2.45

E33   BECKETT, SAMUEL / Waiting For Godot / $1.95 [See also Seven Plays of the Modern Theater, Harold Clurman, ed. GT422 / $4.95]

B79   BEHAN, BRENDAN / The Quare Fellow* and The Hostage**: Two Plays / $2.45 *[See also Seven Plays of the Modern Theater, Harold Clurman, ed. GT422 / $4.95] **[See also Modern British Drama, Henry Popkin, ed. GT614 / $5.95]

GT423   BOWERS, FAUBIAN / Theatre in the East: A Survey of Asian Dance and Drama / $3.95

B117   BRECHT, BERTOLT / The Good Woman of Setzuan / $1.95

B80   BRECHT, BERTOLT / The Jewish Wife and Other Short Plays (In Search of Justice, The Informer, The Elephant Calf, The Measures Taken, The Exception and the Rule, Salzburg Dance of Death) / $1.65

B90   BRECHT, BERTOLT / The Mother / $1.45

B108   BRECHT, BERTOLT / Mother Courage and Her
       Children / $1.50

B333   BRECHT, BERTOLT / The Threepenny Opera / $1.45

GT422 CLURMAN, HAROLD (Ed.) / Seven Plays of the Modern
       Theater / $4.95 (Waiting For Godot by Samuel Beckett, The
       Quare Fellow by Brendan Behan, A Taste of Honey by
       Shelagh Delaney, The Connection by Jack Gelber, The
       Balcony by Jean Genet, Rhinoceros by Eugene Ionesco,
       and The Birthday Party by Harold Pinter)

E159   DELANEY, SHELAGH / A Taste of Honey / $1.95 (See also
       Modern British Drama, Henry Popkin, ed., GT614 / $5.95,
       and Seven Plays of the Modern Theater, Harold Clurman,
       ed. GT422 / $4.95)

E402   DURRENMATT, FRIEDRICH / An Angel Comes to Babylon
       and Romulus the Great / $3.95

E628   DURRENMATT, FRIEDRICH / The Meteor / $1.95

E612   DURRENMATT, FRIEDRICH / Play Strindberg / $1.95

E344   DURRENMATT, FRIEDRICH / The Visit / $2.75

B132   GARSON, BARBARA / MacBird! / $1.95

E223   GELBER, JACK / The Connection / $2.45 [See also Seven
       Plays of the Modern Theater, Harold Clurman, ed.
       GT422 / $4.95]

E130   GENET, JEAN / The Balcony / $2.95 [See also Seven Plays
       of the Modern Theater, Harold Clurman, ed. GT422 / $4.95]

E208   GENET, JEAN / The Blacks: A Clown Show / $2.95

E479   GENET, JEAN / Letters to Roger Blin / $1.95

E577   GENET, JEAN / The Maids and Deathwatch:
       Two Plays / $2.95

E374   GENET, JEAN / The Screens / $1.95

E615   HARRISON, PAUL CARTER (Ed.) / The Kuntu
       Drama / $4.95 (Kabnis by Jean Toomer, A Season in the
       Congo by Aime Cesaire, The Owl Answers and A Beast
       Story by Adrienne Kennedy, Great Goodness of Life by
       Imamu Amiri Baraka (LeRoi Jones), Devil Mas' by Lennox
       Brown, The Sty of the Blind Pig by Phillip Hayes Dean, Mars
       By Clay Goss, The Great MacDaddy by Paul Carter
       Harrison)

E457   HERBERT, JOHN / Fortune and Men's Eyes / $2.95

B154   HOCHHUTH, ROLF / The Deputy / $2.95
B200   HOCHHUTH, ROLF / Soldiers / $1.50
E456   IONESCO, EUGENE / Exit the King / $2.95
E101   IONESCO, EUGENE / Four Plays (The Bald Soprano, The Lesson, The Chairs,* Jack, or The Submission) / $1.95 *[See also Eleven Short Plays of the Modern Theater, Samuel Moon, ed. B107 / $2.45]
E646   IONESCO, EUGENE / A Hell of a Mess / $3.95
E506   IONESCO, EUGENE / Hunger and Thirst and Other Plays / $1.95
E189   IONESCO, EUGENE / The Killer and Other Plays (Improvisation, or The Shepherd's Chameleon, Maid to Marry) / $2.45
E613   IONESCO, EUGENE / Killing Game / $1.95
E259   IONESCO, EUGENE / Rhinoceros* and Other Plays (The Leader, The Future is in Eggs, or It Takes All Sorts to Make a World) / $1.95 *[See also Seven Plays of the Modern Theater, Harold Clurman, ed. GT422 / $4.95]
E485   IONESCO, EUGENE / A Stroll in the Air and Frenzy for Two: Two Plays / $2.45
E119   IONESCO, EUGENE / Three Plays (Amédée, The New Tenant, Victims of Duty) / $2.95
E387   IONESCO, EUGENE / Notes and Counter Notes / $3.95
E496   JARRY, ALFRED / The Ubu Plays / $2.95
E633   LAHR, JOHN (Ed.) / Grove Press Modern Drama / $6.95 (The Caucasian Chalk Circle by Bertolt Brecht, The Toilet by Imamu Amiri Baraka (LeRoi Jones), The White House Murder Case by Jules Feiffer, The Blacks by Jean Genet, Rhinoceros by Eugene Ionesco, Tango by Slawomir Mrozek)
B107   MOON, SAMUEL (Ed.) / One Act: Eleven Short Plays of the Modern Theater / $2.45 (Miss Julie by August Strindberg, Purgatory by William Butler Yeats, The Man With the Flower in His Mouth by Luigi Pirandello, Pullman Car Hiawatha by Thornton Wilder, Hello Out There by William Saroyan, 27 Wagons Full of Cotton by Tennessee Williams, Bedtime Story by Sean O'Casey, Cecile by Jean Anouilh, This Music Crept by Me Upon the Waters by Archibald MacLeish, A Memory of Two Mondays by Arthur Miller, The Chairs by Eugene Ionesco)

E410   MROZEK, SLAWOMIR / Six Plays: The Police, Out at Sea, Enchanted Night, The Party, Charlie, The Martyrdom of Peter Ohey / $2.45

E433   MROZEK, SLAWOMIR / Tango / $1.95

E462   NICHOLS, PETER / Joe Egg / $2.95

E650   NICHOLS, PETER / The National Health / $3.95

E393   ORTON, JOE / Entertaining Mr. Sloane / $2.95

E470   ORTON, JOE / Loot / $1.95

E567   ORTON, JOE / What The Butler Saw / $2.40

E583   OSBORNE, JOHN / Inadmissible Evidence / $2.45

B110   OSBORNE, JOHN / Plays for England and The World of Paul Slickey / $1.45 (The Blood of the Bambergs and Under Plain Cover)

B354   PINTER, HAROLD / Old Times / $1.95

E315   PINTER, HAROLD / The Birthday Party* and The Room: Two Plays / $1.95 *[See also Seven Plays of the Modern Theater, Harold Clurman, ed. GT422 / $4.95]

E299   PINTER, HAROLD / The Caretaker* and The Dumb Waiter: Two Plays / $1.95 *[See also Modern British Drama, Henry Popkin, ed. GT422 / $5.95]

E411   PINTER, HAROLD / The Homecoming / $1.95

E432   PINTER, HAROLD / The Lover, Tea Party, The Basement: Three Plays / $1.95

E480   PINTER, HAROLD / A Night Out, Night School, Revue Sketcı s: Early Plays / $1.95

GT614   POPKIN, HENRY (Ed.) / Modern British Drama / $5.95 (A Taste of Honey by Shelagh Delaney, The Hostage by Brendan Behan, Roots by Arnold Wesker, Serjeant Musgrave's Dance by John Arden, One Way Pendulum by N. F. Simpson, The Caretaker by Harold Pinter)

E635   SHEPARD, SAM / The Tooth of Crime and Geography of a Horsedreamer / $3.95

E626   STOPPARD, TOM / Jumpers / $1.95

B319   STOPPARD, TOM / Rosencrantz and Guilderstern Are Dead / $1.95

E660   STOREY, DAVID / In Celebration / $2.95

E62   WALEY, ARTHUR (Translator) / The No Plays of Japan / $3.95

GROVE PRESS, INC., 196 West Houston St., New York, N.Y. 10014

Other Grove Press Paperbacks

☐ ALLEN, DONALD M., ed. *The New American Poetry.*
E237/$3.95
☐ ARSAN, EMMANUELLE. *Emmanuelle.* B361/$1.95
☐ BECKETT, SAMUEL. *Three Novels. Molloy; Malone Dies; The Unnamable.* B78/$1.95
—*Waiting for Godot.* E33/$1.95
☐ BERNE, ERIC, M.D. *Games People Play.* B186/$1.95
☐ BRAUTIGAN, RICHARD. *A Confederate General from Big Sur.* B283/$1.50
☐ BRECHT, BERTOLT. *Galileo.* B120/$1.95
—*Mother Courage and Her Children.* B108/$1.50
☐ BURROUGHS, WILLIAM S. *Naked Lunch.* B115/$1.95
☐ CUMMINGS, E. E. *100 Selected Poems.* E190/$1.95
☐ FANON, FRANTZ. *The Wretched of the Earth.* B342/$1.95
☐ GENET, JEAN. *The Balcony.* E130/$2.95
☐ IONESCO, EUGENE. *Four Plays. The Bald Soprano; The Lesson; The Chairs; Jack, or The Submission.* E101/$1.95
☐ KEROUAC, JACK. *The Subterraneans.* B300/$1.50
☐ LAWRENCE, D. H. *Lady Chatterley's Lover.* B9/$1.95
☐ MALCOLM X. *Autobiography of Malcolm X.* B146/$1.95
☐ MILLER, HENRY. *Tropic of Cancer.* B10/$1.95
—*Tropic of Capricorn.* B59/$1.95
☐ PINTER, HAROLD. *The Homecoming.* E411/$1.95
☐ REAGE, PAULINE. *Story of O* (film ed.). B396/$1.95
☐ SNOW, EDGAR. *Red Star Over China.* E618/$3.95
☐ STOPPARD, TOM. *Rosencrantz & Guildenstern Are Dead.* B319/$1.95
—*Travesties.* E661/$1.95
☐ TRUFFAUT, FRANCOIS. *The Story of Adele H.* B395/$2.45

At your bookstore, or order below.

Grove Press, Inc., 196 West Houston St., New York, N.Y. 10014.

Please mail me the books checked above. I am enclosing $_____
(No COD. Add 35¢ per book for postage and handling.)

Name _____

Address _____

City_____State_____Zip_____